CW80548997

LIBERATION

LIBERATION

FREEDOM FROM YOUR BIGGEST BLOCK TO PURE JOY

Sondra Ray
&
Markus Ray

Immortal Ray Productions

Nashville   Washington D.C.

OTHER BOOKS BY SONDRA RAY

- ❖ Rebirthing in the New Age
- ❖ I Deserve Love
- ❖ Loving Relationships I
- ❖ The Only Diet There Is
- ❖ Celebration of Breath
- ❖ Ideal Birth
- ❖ Drinking the Divine
- ❖ Pure Joy
- ❖ Inner Communion
- ❖ How To Be Chic, Fabulous, and Live Forever
- ❖ Interlude With the Gods
- ❖ Loving Relationships II
- ❖ Essays on Creating Sacred Relationships
- ❖ Healing and Holiness
- ❖ Pele's Wish
- ❖ Relationships Treasury
- ❖ Rock Your World with the Divine Mother
- ❖ Liberation Breathing: The Divine Mother's Gift
- ❖ Spiritual intimacy: What You Really Want with a Mate
- ❖ Babaji: My Miraculous Meetings with a Maha Avatar
- ❖ Physical Immortality: How to Overcome Death
- ❖ Lately I've Been Thinking

OTHER BOOKS BY MARKUS RAY

- ❖ Liberation Breathing: The Divine Mother's Gift
- ❖ Odes to the Divine Mother
- ❖ Miracles with My Master, Tara Singh
- ❖ Babaji: My Miraculous Meetings With A Maha Avatar
- ❖ The Master is Beautiful
- ❖ Little Ganesh Book
- ❖ A Painter's Life (in progress)

IMMORTAL RAY PRODUCTIONS
301 TINGEY STREET, SE #338
WASHINGTON DC, 20003

Immortal Ray Productions
Nashville   Washington D.C.

Library of Congress Cataloging in Publication Data

Ray, Sondra; Lately I've Been Thinking

I. Relationships. 2. Self-Mastery. 3. Life Wisdom

Cover Design: Markus Ray
Frontispiece Image: Judy Totton Photography of London
Back Cover Image: Judy Totton Photography of London.

ISBN 13: Paperback 978-1-950684-00-7
ISBN 13: E-Book   978-1-950684-01-4

DEDICATION

To all Liberation Breathing Practitioners, Breathworkers, and Rebirthers around the world, we dedicate this book to you who have given your life to awakening people to their brightest and best Self—through the conscious use of their own breath. Taking people from the darkness to the light is nothing short of liberating people from the lies held lodged in their subconscious mind. The work we do to awaken the truth ultimately results in overcoming sorrow and death. This book is for you, and all people who have taken a breath to free themselves from the traumas of their past. May this book bring you Liberation, even more, and place you in the Truth, Love and Simplicity of Pure Joy.

"I RULE MY MIND, WHICH I ALONE MUST RULE."

Lesson # 236 in the Workbook of *A Course in Miracles.*

CONTENTS

FOREWORD

It is a great privilege for me to write the Foreword to Sondra Ray's newest book on *Personal Lies*, **Liberation: Freedom from Your Biggest Block to Pure Joy.** I have known Sondra for 37 years. She has been the biggest influence in my life besides my family. She gave me the best career and life purpose I could ever have imagined. She taught me to do only the things I love to do. Traveling the world teaching Breathwork, Rebirthing, Liberation Breathing, The Loving Relationships Training, Sexuality Workshops, and Spiritual Healing Seminars has been the most amazing adventure and wonderful surprise that I have been given, and privileged to give back in divine service.

This book is a Road Map to unravel your mind, and to see the main subconscious script by which you have been living your life. It is a Road Map to Healing. The *Personal Lie* is the biggest saboteur that rules your life as it is today. Unexamined and unchanged, this thought is on an endless *mental loop* that can ruin your life. I thank Babaji for bringing Sondra into my life 37 years ago to point this *Personal Lie* out to me. Without this deep life wisdom I would not have the deeper understanding I have about the important events in my life.

My *Personal Lie* is, "I am the opposite of what my parents wanted." They had 2 girls already and wanted a boy—especially my father. When I was born at home, he initially was disappointed for 7 seconds, then he was happy I was a healthy girl. So the lie I had was, "I am the opposite of what they wanted as a woman," and, "I'm a disappointment." In my life I was a rebel always doing the opposite of what people expected from me—then I disappointed them, or I was disappointed. I even chose the opposite man to marry than I wanted. I had a choice between my high school/college boyfriend of 5 years, and Michael who I dated for about 6 months. I choose the wrong one.

In 1979 I was in India with my husband Michael and 2 children, 9 months and 4 years old. My husband wanted to go see Rajneesh in India. We had a sexuality issue and had taken a Tantric Workshop from his followers. Thinking he could "solve our problem," we spent a brief period of time in his ashram in Poona, then decided to leave Rajneesh and travel around India. On the train I was reading Yogananda's book, *The*

Autobiography of a Yogi, and to my surprise I discovered Babaji. I wanted to go find Him. I was determined. It was as if I was being called.

Herakhan, Babaji's home in the foothills of the Himalayas, is difficult to find. But we blundered into taxi drivers who brought us to the right place. They took us as far as they could go, then we had to put the kids on mules and hike up the river bed. We were exhausted when we finally arrived in Herakhan. Babaji Himself greeted us and told us to sit by the fire near the river and rest. We had not let anyone know we were coming. We just showed up. There were several other new arrivals who Babaji actually sent away. I was afraid He would tell us to go. I was surprised when He told us we were undisciplined, which we were, but that we could stay so the kids could recover. He loved children. He was childlike Himself, and playful, young at heart. He gave the children a lot of attention. I felt an immediate connection to Babaji, and I loved how He treated my children.

Then we had to climb the 108 steps to the Ashram and Temple area. Babaji led us to the Temple and told us that would be where we would sleep. Surprised again, it was the *opposite* of what I expected. The next time we saw Babaji was before the evening chanting. He looked at how we placed our belongings, then told us to take everything over to the *opposite* side of where He first told us to go. He was processing my *opposite case* with a leela, before I even knew leelas existed. A leela is a divine lesson the Guru puts you through in order for you to overcome a major piece of your case, or mental "tendency." Mine was, "I am the opposite of what people want." He was certainly bringing that to my attention, big time.

We did Chanting, Fire Ceremony, and Karma Yoga for three days. This was how long we were allowed to stay. It felt like a lifetime. Every day with Babaji burns off 9 years of Karma and crud. I was 27 years old. Leonard Orr was there with several of his Rebirthers. I was intrigued by Rebirthing but never got to try it. My son had crossed eyes—and I realized they crossed because Michael and I were going in *opposite* directions. Before we left, Babaji pulled me aside and told me, "Why are you following him when he should be following you?"

We traveled for 5 months all over India, Sri Lanka, Nepal and the Philippines. We even trekked to the Base Camp of Mount Everest. It was so scary watching Sherpas carry the kids over wobbly wooden bridges.

When we got back to the USA, I took what Babaji said seriously and divorced Michael. I moved to Westwood, California, and worked for my dad. He often mistakenly called me his son, in the office. I was being processed again on my *opposite* case. I loved my dad for helping me out at the time. We really had a lot of healing in that period.

One day I walked into the Sisterhood Book Store, and as I was walking down the aisle a book flew off the shelf and hit me on the shoulder—it was **Loving Relationships** by Sondra Ray. Thank you Babaji! I immediately knew I needed that book and bought it. I read the book in one day as I felt it spoke directly to me. I knew everything in it was true. The book and Sondra Ray really resonated with the core of my being.

I have a Master's Degree in Early Childhood Psychology. Several years after I finished my degree I worked in a few really good preschool facilities—started by doctors for their practice. I wrote my Master's thesis on "Self-Esteem in Young Children." I had developed a Self-Esteem Test, where the children would point to a Happy Face, Sad Face, or Angry Face to represent how they felt about themselves, their parents, their teachers, their siblings, and their friends. I was very surprised to discover that very young children had very low Self-Esteem. When I read Sondra's book, **Loving Relationships**, I realized that we have preverbal decisions we made about ourselves and our life from our conception, womb and birth. I understood why very young children do not feel happy about themselves.

After reading **Loving Relationships** I immediately wanted to take the training. I found it was being given in Los Angeles. When I discovered the cost for the seminar I thought it was too expensive—I didn't believe I was good enough to spend that much money on myself. In 1982 I started Rebirthing instead of taking the LRT, what I really wanted to do. After I had several sessions I realized I never gave myself what I really wanted. I decided to give myself the greatest gift, ever, the LRT. As soon as I made the commitment to myself I created all the money.

Sondra Ray was my first Trainer. After I took the training I transformed so much in one weekend, that I enrolled 18 people in the next training a couple of months later. My parents, my sister, and most of my friends saw such a change in me they wanted to experience the training as well.

Not long after my second training, Sondra published **The Only Diet There Is.** I knew that we needed this seminar in Los Angeles that is so beauty and weight conscious. I tracked Sondra down in Hawaii and invited her to do the first "The Only Diet There Is" seminar in LA. She agreed to do it. We had over 50 people come to a Hotel in Westwood, around the corner from my home! The seminar was about Forgiveness, and letting go of old thoughts about food and your body. Sondra did a lecture, processes, and we had a lot of sharing. Then everyone laid down for a group Rebirth. There was a lot of letting go, breathing, crying, sweating and even throwing up. Back then people were more dramatic about their process. The results were amazing—right in that evening people dropped 5-10 pounds. I really saw the power of the breath, changing thoughts and Forgiveness.

Sondra was not happy with her LA organizers and wanted me to become the LA Organizer for the LRT. I was not a Rebirther yet, however, I had started to date a man who had been Rebirthing since the beginning. I accepted the challenge. Sondra was staying with me. When we came home from shopping we found a blue telegram from India, stuck in my front window screen. It was from Babaji. It said, "Congratulations, you finally got it right in Los Angeles. Babaji."

Amazing we had Babaji's blessing for the new LA LRT Center. We always had very successful workshops with 100-200 people. My relationships didn't make it for me, but our business flourished. I was always told my case was hard to crack around my *Personal Lie*.

Every time a new LRT trainer came to town they suggested a different *Personal Lie* for me. Bob Mandel thought it was, "I am a disappointment as a woman." He did give me one of my favorite Eternal Truths, the opposite of the *Personal Lie*. "*I, Rhonda, am a surprisingly wonderful woman."* I still use this one today. Another trainer thought it was, "I am wrong as a woman." So my Eternal Truth, "I am right as a woman." Another trainer thought it was, "I am unwanted as a woman." This Eternal Truth would be, "I am wanted as a woman." One Trainer even thought it was, "I am confused as a woman," because everyone was confused about my *Personal Lie.* I did attract people that were confused about their sexuality. I even dated a few Gay men.

After Sondra stayed with me for awhile, she thought I did everything *opposite* than the way she would do it. She thought my *PL* was, "I am opposite as a woman." When Sondra asked me to write this Foreword, she reminded me of this *Personal Lie*, which even Babaji was processing me on 40 years ago. Our *Personal Lie* can be very tricky and often people work on the *results* of the *Personal Lie*, instead of the real *Personal Lie* itself. The *Personal Lie* is the bottom thought, the foundation that all negative thoughts build on. For example, "I am opposite of what my parents wanted a girl, instead of a boy," therefore I create disappointment in me or I am disappointed by the results I'm receiving.

I remember getting this with Sondra shopping in Beverly Hills where I grew up. I had never spent more than $100 on a dress. We were looking for a dress for my 20th Beverly Hills High School Reunion. Everything I liked

Sondra didn't. We went into an expensive store on Rodeo Drive. Sondra said, "I found the perfect dress for you!" It was a black velvet dress. It was 50% off—but still $750. I bought it, and my Self-Esteem really increased that day, knowing I deserved the best. I still have that dress and it still fits!

When Sondra reminded me recently that, "I'm the opposite," was my *Personal Lie*, I couldn't even think of the opposite for the Eternal Truth. I knew she was right since I couldn't even figure it out. She gave me the affirmation, "I, Rhonda, am now a compatible, wanted woman." I told her I had been on dating sites for the last couple of years and had been attracting men who were scammers, or the *opposite* politically from me. Sondra gave me the affirmation, "I, Rhonda, am now attracting a compatible, available man who fascinates me." This last ten days I have been writing these affirmations 20 times, 3 times a day. I also swam a mile a day breathing the affirmations into my body. I have also been using Mala beads to say Om Namah Shivaya, 108 times, X 10, plus a Divine Mother Mantra AMMA gave me 16 years ago. I saw AMMA in Atlanta this year which reconnected me to my 2 mantras—one from her and one from Babaji. Sondra saw AMMA this year in Washington DC. I think AMMA and Babaji wanted us to get back connected. We are definitely Soul Sisters.

I feel really good with both these affirmations I have been working on, I feel they are integrated in my body. I am expecting the new compatible man to show up!

In 1989 Sondra encouraged me to write a book on healing sexuality issues as a follow up to *I Deserve Love*. You always teach what you need to learn. Through Rebirthing and the LRT I went from non-orgasmic to having Blissful Tantric Sex. I published **Sexual Evolution** in 1991, still available on E-Bay. I led workshops on sexuality, doing research for this book with my husband for 18 years, Jeffrey Baker. We taught how your conception, womb, and birth thoughts—or *Birth Script*— affect your sexuality. We saw people's biggest problem with sex was always a result of their *Personal Lies.*

So if you want a great blissful sex-life, prosperity, living your true purpose, read this book, do all the processes, and unravel your case. We are all unique, and every one of us has the *right* to Perfect Happiness. My favorite lesson in *A Course In Miracles* is #101, "God's Will for me is Perfect Happiness." By discovering our *Personal Lie* and transforming it to our Eternal Truth, we are dissolving our EGO, which then leads to Perfect Happiness. We are all entitled to this miracle! Thank you Sondra Ray for all your contributions to my life of Perfect Happiness!

Love, Rhonda Levand

Acknowledgements

We would like to acknowledge the original Rebirthing Founder, Leonard Orr, who opened our minds to the *Personal Lie*, our most dominant negative thought in our subconscious mind, sabotaging our life. We would also express gratitude for Rebirthing itself, the process of deep connected Energy Breathing that Leonard taught us back in 1974 to help clear this main saboteur. We have been practitioners of this good work ever since. We acknowledge the Divine Mother, who guided us to actively include Her Energy in the Rebirthing / Breathwork process, which we now call Liberation Breathing®: The Divine Mother's Gift. We acknowledge all those who helped us prepare this manuscript. You know who you are. Lastly, we acknowledge all our breathwork clients, colleagues, and breathers around the world who inspired us to put together this book to define the *Personal Lie*, and help people find certain Liberation from it.

PREFACE

Those of us committed to Liberation Breathing / Rebirthing / Breathwork have found that discovering our *Personal Lie* (most dominant negative consciousness factor in the subconscious) made all the difference in the world in sorting out our lives. It was like finding the magic key that kind of explained everything for us. So then we began helping clients find theirs right off the bat in the first session of breathwork. This gave them so much understanding about their situations, past and present, and so much relief. It takes a skilled breathworker to locate this *lie* and to help the client release it. Markus and I realized that more people outside of breathwork in the general public need to know about this. So that is the reason for this book.

As far as I know, I am the only Rebirther in the world who kept a running list of *Personal Lies* that I encountered with clients. So obviously I am the one to write this book. When you are aware of your own *Personal Lie*, you can see how it affects your relationship, your career, your body and everything. It is a real *Liberation* to understand this. Getting over it can be tricky. That is because it is an addiction. One may have had it for decades, or from birth, or even from a past life. So therefore you don't get over your *Personal Lie* overnight. In this book we try to help people get over it faster. However, they need to work on themselves and we cannot do that work for them. Our job is to help them discover it and tell them what we ourselves have done to release it.

Most people in the *main stream world* have no idea that this thought is running their life. If they are lucky enough to get to a breathworker, and if they are lucky enough to get a breathworker who handles this area, then they have a good chance to get liberated from their *Personal Lie*. But people who have never found a breathworker are going to be in the dark about all this. So this book is for you to get exposed to such important information. Hopefully you will get a glimpse of your *Personal Lie*, and then have a breathwork session after reading this book— as the *Personal Lie* must be *breathed out* of the cellular memories in which it is lodged.

There are some breathworkers who have not been trained in this area. So you need to make sure you get one who deals with this issue. I have not trained all the breathworkers who are practicing out there. But believe me, those who have been trained by me know how to process a person's *Personal Lie*, with this a major part of their training. It is my opinion that breathworkers who do not deal with the *Personal Lie* and Liberation from it are not fully trained.

I was one of the very first practitioners of Rebirthing in the world. I helped the founder, Leonard Orr, develop it in 1974, and spread it around the world—something I am still doing. Later my husband Markus and I added a more spiritual development to the work. We do the breathing the same way as we did in the beginning. But near the end of the session we have added the reading of the Divine Mother names while the client is still breathing. Then we have the client turn on their side and switch to nasal breathing and we say a very, very powerful Divine Mother mantra for completion. The Divine Mother finishes the job of the Liberation. That is why we call it Liberation Breathing now. It is still the original Rebirthing Breath I received from Leonard Orr back in 1974, but this added completion with the Divine Mother, we were told, makes the session 9X more powerful. Our clients confirm this with their miraculous stories and results.

Breathwork itself is very liberating. That is why I have dedicated my whole life to this work which I have been doing for over 45 years. But to have the help of the Divine Mother is a lot more liberating. Liberation is why we are here, one could argue, in defining our Life's purpose. We hope you will try a Liberation Breathing session one day. We and other certified Liberation Breathing Practitioners are also available via Skype or Zoom for sessions. *Bit.ly/LBPractitioner*

It is our wish that you have Liberation from your *Personal Lie.* It is an invalidation of your personal Divinity. It is a major cause of low self-esteem. It explains why one's behavior is the way it is. It is often the cause of failure; of relationships problems; of depression; and of stress and illnesses. So I wanted this book to improve your life, your relationships, your mind and your body. And I am sure, if you read the whole thing, you will understand why I was the one who had to write it.

When you do the five questions and review the long list of over 350 *Personal Lies* I have gathered over the years, you should be able to locate your specific *Personal Lie.* If you think you have one not on my list, I would surely like to know about it. So please email me at Immortalray@earthlink.net. If you feel confused which it is, please schedule a session with us or one of our Certified LB Practitioners so we can help you figure out yours. It is very important to get the exact right one. There may be several affecting you and you do need to change all of those thoughts. However, there is always one that is the most dominate—and you have to be certain about it. The more certain you are, the quicker it will be to forgive it and release it from its effects on your life.

Once you are sure about it, you will see how it has been affecting your relationships, your career, your family dynamics, your general moods in life, etc. It kind of "explains" why things have turned out the way they have for you.

I am excited for you to get clear on this as I know for sure you will be very grateful and you will start to have a whole new life.

Love,   *Sondra Ray*

INTRODUCTION

Liberation is the name of this book, and the name of the type of Breathing we represent. We teach and practice Liberation Breathing® internationally. "Liberation from what?" you might ask. We see people all around the globe in our work. We notice people are not really experiencing Pure Joy in their lives, even though they are actively in pursuit of happiness. There is a Joy that is blocked by a compendium of subconscious thoughts—major saboteurs—and liberation from these is the main focus of this work: **Liberation: Freedom From Your Biggest Block to Pure Joy.** The main one of these saboteurs we call a *Personal Lie*. It is your biggest block to Pure Joy. It is underlying all the rest, so if we can help you be free of that one block, then many others—that are corollaries to this *one block*—will simply fade away.

A Course in Miracles, which we study closely in our work, mentions that miracles are necessary for us to, "remove the blocks to the awareness of love's presence." *(ACIM;*

Text; Introduction) In a Divine Existence that only knows of absolute peace and joy, anything not supremely happy is a block to this natural inheritance. Pure Joy is pushed from view by the *Personal Lie.* It is mostly unexamined, therefore it remains intact within the subterranean regions of our mind—yet, nevertheless active in giving us a Life of so-so experiences and results. Many of us spent at least sometime in a blue period of questioning, and far from being supremely happy, we felt caught in a situation of disillusionment, grief, or inescapable depression. Statistically, depression affects 6-7% of the US population per year. That is 16.2 million people, estimated; so the figure is probably double that, as most people who are depressed usually bite the bullet, march on with a stiff upper lip, and simply bear it as *normal.* And though not affected presently, the millions who have suffered a low mood at some point in their life would most likely be staggering, if the statistics were kept.

We hear a lot about people's problems in our work as Liberation Breathing Practitioners. They seem myriad. But most are traceable to one: Separation from our Source— or, our imagined separation from our Source. It's impossible to really be separated from this Source, because it is what gives us Life. To be separated from it, we would have to be dead. And even if we choose to leave our body, we are still connected to the Infinite Unified Field of Everything, therefore still never truly separated from our Source. So the "problem" has really been solved, but we forget this solution. Instead, the principle way we maintain our sense of separation from our Source is with a negative thought, lodged in our subconscious mind, not brought to question. It is not a true thought, but we think that it is. This is why we call this thought a *Personal Lie*. It is your worst dominant thought in your collection of low self-esteem thoughts. It is the basis of your belief in separation from your Source. It is a "false self-identity" you made up to replace the True Self-Identity your Source created. It is a thought that leads to conflict, sorrow and death instead of one that leads to more Peace, Joy, and Immortal Life.

One could define the Source simply as an Energy of Pure Joy. How did we drift so far afield from this Primordial Energy of all pervasive happiness?

Many people we see are naturally productive people, and have a good sense of self-esteem. They tend to be positive by nature, and have breezed through their lives without much drama or struggle. They might say, "Well, I don't have many negative thoughts, and if I do, I don't dwell on them." This is GOOD! Wonderful. But we have a saying, "Unless you are like Jesus or Babaji or the Divine Mother, raising the dead or walking on water, you still have something to clear." There is always something higher in our evolutionary journey to full Enlightenment and Awakening. What would this book have for these people? There could be fine tuning that will make your life flow even better, serve even greater levels of good, and make your life even more a blessing to yourself and those around you. Not that we are promoting "self-improvement." We are not promoting anything except removing all of the *shadows* that may be in the way of you realizing the effulgent Light you already are. And the *Personal Lie* is one of these major *shadows* whose time has come to be shone away.

The *false you* vs. the *Real You*—this is the battleground upon which the personal conflicts of our ego wage war. Liberating yourself from the conflicts of your life and awakening more Peace and Joy of the Real You is the purpose of this little book. You may already be well on your way, or you may not have even started this introspective journey to the deeper Peace and Joy within. It does not matter where you are, this work with the *Personal Lie* will shed light on your Life—no matter where you are along the way in this evolutionary dawn of waking up!

We have collected over 350 *Personal Lies*. Just when we think we have "heard them all," someone comes forth with a nuance of their "case"—as we call their personal history of negative thoughts that keep them stuck—that sheds light on their particular conflict or block.

Uncovering the *Personal Lie* is the first major step in the process of healing of it. Once you see it, and how it was made, and how it was acted out and maintained, its correction is already well on its way to changing the course of your Life or the better. You just "look at it," without judging it. We have listed over 350 *Personal Lies* we collected in Chapter 1. And, we have given you a fool proof set of five questions to ask yourself to locate yours. Between answering honestly the questions, and reviewing the *Personal Lie* list, you should have no trouble uncovering and locating yours. We are also available for consultations and Liberation Breathing sessions here: **bit.ly/LBSession** if you get stuck.

LOVE,   *Markus Ray*

LIBERATION

Chapter 1.

YOUR BIGGEST BLOCK

What if there was one place everyone was stuck and you found out what that was and you changed it in yourself? Would you not be interested? What if you could remove any block you ever will have to experiencing Pure Joy all of the time—in short *your heaven on earth*?

After doing Liberation Breathwork on thousands of people I can tell you that every person is stuck in the same place. The only being that I know who would not be stuck in that is Babaji Himself—my Master. Why? He was not even born of a woman. He materialized His body; therefore, He has no birth trauma. The rest of us have a birth trauma; and with that we all dragged in one key negative thought that is constantly sabotaging everything. It affects your self-esteem. It affects your body. It affects

1

your relationships. It affects your career. It affects your finances. It affects everything.

The problem is that this thought is in the subconscious and very suppressed. How can you heal it if you don't even know what it is? It is a pre-verbal thought. It formed before you even had language in this life to define it. The other problem is this: It is a negative thought you have that has become an addiction. Most people never even find out what it is. And how do you deal with addictions? Not easy. First of all, you need a skilled person to point it out to you. Second of all, you need a technique to release that thought, that addiction.

So, what am I talking about? Don't worry, I won't leave you in the dark. I intend to expose it all completely in this little book. What I am talking about is what we breathworkers call your *Personal Lie*. It amounts to your most negative thought about yourself. You might think you already know it; however, since it is buried in the subconscious, just guessing what it is not enough. You need someone who can process you perfectly. You may have several negative thoughts about yourself. But you need to find out the KEY one that is the most dominate consciousness factor you have. The reason it is called a *Personal Lie* is because God did not create you with that thought. You made it up in some life time based on your experience. Or you made it up at your birth. But it is likely that you may have had it for many lifetimes. Therefore, it is definitely an addiction!

Those of us who have uncovered our *Personal Lies* are grateful, yes. But we can tell you it is not so easy to change it and drop it. The ego wants to hang on to it. It is also familiar and there is likely to be a fear of even giving up what is familiar. Once in India, I was at the fire ceremony and a student from Estonia approached me asking this: "Sondra is it possible to give up your *Personal Lie* in this lifetime?" I totally understood her dilemma. I understood her desperation. I opened my mouth and what came out for an answer was this: "Only by the help of God". That is of course, true of giving up most addictions. You need a higher power.

I think I am the only breathworker in the world who has kept a list of different *Personal Lies* I have uncovered in my practice. I am going to list them all so you really get what I am talking about. Probably one of these is yours and it will stand out and it will explain why your life has been how it has been. To my great surprise, I continually find new ones, which is almost unbelievable to me. I think I have heard them all, and lo and behold—there is a new one. If you have one that is not on this list, I certainly want to know about it !!

PERSONAL LIES I HAVE COLLECTED:

1. I am not good enough
2. I am bad
3. I am wrong
4. I am a disappointment
5. I can't
6. I don't want to be here
7. I am a failure
8. I am weak
9. I am guilty
10. I am not perfect
11. I am nothing
12. I don't matter
13. I am not worthy
14. I am worthless
15. I am not lovable
16. I am not important
17. I hurt people
18. I am a burden
19. I should not be here
20. I am a fake
21. I am a lie
22. I am a fraud
23. I am a shock
24. I am empty
25. I am too much
26. I am invisible

27. I am alone
28. I am not wanted
29. I am a killer
30. I cause problems
31. I cause pain
32. I am not enough
33. I ruin things
34. I am a mistake
35. I am not complete
36. I am ugly
37. I am stupid
38. I am destructive
39. I am stuck
40. I don't exist
41. I am dirty/ filthy
42. I am an interference
43. I am not able
44. I am not capable
45. I am different
46. I am not the one
47. I am a replacement
48. I am incongruent
49. I am not dignified
50. I am an impostor
51. I am dangerous
52. I am a secret
53. I am nearly dead
54. I am dead

55. I am a mystery

56. I'm not ready

57. I'm to blame

58. I have something wrong with me

59. I'm not OK

60. I am an embarrassment

61. I am not wanted as a woman/man

62. I am not here

63. I am not acceptable

64. I am not acceptable as a woman

65. I am not legal

66. I am not wise

67. I am a devil

68. I am the wrong one

69. I am a loser

70. I am inappropriate

71. I am flawed

72. I am a gangster

73. I am not the right one

74. I am the wrong sex

75. I am illegitimate

76. I am not who I am

77. I am sneaky

78. I am impure

79. I am useless

80. I am a criminal

81. I am in the way

82. I am a freak

83. I am not the best

84. I am not authentic

85. I am a coward

86. I am a heretic

87. I am mediocre

88. I am a menace

89. I am pathetic

90. I am a monster

91. I am a disaster

92. I am clumsy

93. I am a trickster

94. I am inferior

95. I am not welcome

96. I am a "let down"

97. I can't make it

98. I am an intrusion

99. I am a threat

100. I am a waste of space

101. I am not necessary

102. I am a con man

103. I am foolish

104. I am boring

105. I am disgusting

106. I am tainted

107. I am disposable/discarded

108. I am weird

109. I am condemned

110. I am a slut

111. I am a pervert
112. I am pointless
113. I am ridiculous
114. I am unsafe
115. I am a sham
116. I am a stranger
117. I am horrible
118. I am irrelevant
119. I am damaged
120. I am trouble
121. I am not brave
122. I am an obstacle
123. I am trapped
124. I am ineffective
125. I am wicked
126. I am lost
127. I am timid
128. I am fragile
129. I am strange
130. I am dishonest
131. I am disconnected
132. I am a mess
133. I am extreme
134. I am evil
135. I am defeated
136. I am hurt
137. I don't know
138. I am unclear

139. I am not needed

140. I am difficult

141. I am broken

142. I am damned

143. I am devious

144. I am shut down

145. I am distant

146. I am marked for death

147. I am a screw-up

148. I am an idiot

149. I am not pleasing

150. I am unholy

151. I am an abomination

152. I am doomed

153. I am not all here

154. I am another person

155. I am someone else

156. I am hurtful

157. I am poison

158. I am mean

159. I am a rebel

160. I am unstable

161. I am second rate

162. I am impossible

163. I am careless

164. I am cursed

165. I am closed

166. I am not here for me

167. I am not wanted for me

168. I am **a se**ductress

169. I am a bitch

170. I am garbage

171. I am crap

172. I am a disturbance

173. I have no value

174. I am the opposite

175. I am cut off

176. I am not likeable

177. I am unsure

178. I am less than

179. I am withdrawn

180. I am a disgrace

181. I am a cheat

182. I am rotten

183. I am the darkness

184. I am crazy

185. I am lacking

186. I am a hindrance

187. I am the last

188. I am toxic

189. I am not good enough for God

190. I am a thief

191. I am an outsider

192. I am dark

193. I am below everyone else

194. I am always on my own

195. I ruin people's lives

196. I am complicated

197. I am the worst

198. I am held back

199. I am contrary

200. I am too fast

201. I am tarnished

202. I am on my own

203. I can't live

204. I am a black witch

205. I am not suitable to live

206. I am an illusion

207. I am not of any influence

208. I am used goods

209. I am selfish

210. I am elsewhere

211. I am an invader

212. I am insignificant

213. I might be cruel

214. I am one too much

215. I am a bastard

216. I am untimely

217. I am irresponsible

218. I am in prison

219. I mess things up

220. I am despicable

221. I can't survive

222. I want to die

223. I am leftover
224. I am dead weight
225. I am a fool
226. I am a betrayer
227. I am a punishment for my mother
228. I am abandoned
229. I am denied
230. I am a suspect
231. I am a misfit
232. I am nasty
233. I am unprotected
234. I am an abuser
235. I am crude
236. I cannot be myself
237. I am limited
238. I am hopeless
239. I am slow
240. I am not divine
241. I can't win
242. I am guilty for having it all
243. I am not nice
244. I am not reliable
245. I am covert
246. I am worse than the devil
247. I am only just average
248. I am not free
249. I cannot win as a woman
250. I am in a fog

251. I am death itself

252. I am in limbo

253. I am not myself

254. I am hypocrite

255. I am deprived

256. I am creepy

257. I am a lost cause

258. I am blocked

259. I am a slave

260. I am a flop

261. I am washed up

262. I am a problem

263. I am a swindler

264. I can't be who I am

265. I am bad news

266. I am not part of this world

267. I am not expected

268. I am cheated

269. I am conflicted

270. I am an assassin

271. I am on hold

272. I should be thrown away

273. I am a blob

274. I am a demon

275. I am a bother

276. I am a vampire

277. I am stopped before I start

278. I am a parasite

279. My life is not my own
280. I am exhausting
281. I am a tyrant
282. I am tough
283. I am manipulated
284. I am a manipulator
285. I am frustrated
286. I am not the one I should be
287. I am hollow
288. I have to fight to live
289. I am naive
290. I am not sharp enough
291. I am violent
292. I am not suitable for life
293. I am uncertain
294. I am not good for anything
295. I am depleted
296. I am bad for being good
297. I am cut off
298. I am a fallen angel
299. I am displeasing to God
300. I am not secure
301. I have nothing to offer
302. I am apathetic
303. I am complacent
304. I am a distraction
305. I am bad blood
306. I am asleep

307. I am not aligned

308. I am disobedient

309. I am at fault

310. I am a felon

311. I am not satisfactory

312. I am forgotten

313. I am a disturbance

314. I am left out

315. I am dark

316. I am annoying

317. I am undesirable

318. I can't be happy as a woman

319. I am a punishment

320. I am a target

321. I am aimless

322. I am overbearing

323. I am left behind

324. I am shut down

325. I am not worth anything

326. I am irrelevant

327. I am dreadful

328. I am in a shell

329. I am indecisive

330. I am born to suffer

331. I am poisonous

332. I am a refugee

333. I cannot cope

334. I am unforgivable

335. I am depleted

336. I am obstructed

337. I am an asshole

338. I am ambivalent

339. I am a slave

340. I am contaminated

341. I am awkward

342. I am discard-able

343. I am deformed

344. I am hidden

345. I am fragile

346. I am nobody

347. I am scary

348. I am not worth loving

349. I am gross

350. I am defective

351. I am disregarded

352. I am intimidating

353. I am a troublemaker

354. I am a destroyer

355. I am brutal

356. I am entangled

357. I am defiant

358. I am a deviant

359. I am explosive

360. I am chaotic

361. I am not sustainable

362. I am confused

363. I am hated by God
364. I am guarded
365. I am impotent

As you can see, there are a lot of negative thoughts stored down there in our subconscious minds! You would be surprised how people resist looking at their *Personal Lie* –even though their life is not going well. They have no idea their deepest negative judgment about themselves is affecting them so much. And they may be resisting the basic metaphysical fact that their own thoughts are what are being projected outward, even from the part of their mind that is subconscious, and producing ALL OF THEIR RESULTS. They are responsible for everything that happens to them. In other words, there are no victims, ever, just *cause and effect* relationships. This is another name for "karma"—the cause-and-effect results of your thoughts, the worst being your *Personal Lie*.

HOW DO I FIND OUT MY PERSONAL LIE?

Here is the way you can find out yours. Write out the answer to these questions below in a complete sentence that starts with "I." If you get the same answer several times, that is probably IT. If you get five different answers, figure out which one is the worst of the five. Which one sort of explains your life? Which one do you react to the most? Which one defines your Life?

A. My most negative thought about myself is
_____.

B. The reason my life does not work perfectly all
the time is _____.

C. What I am afraid people will find out about me
is that I _____.

D. The most negative thought I formed about
myself at my birth was _____.

E. My absolute worst thought about myself is
_____.

Okay, which answer is repeated several times? That is
probably the one. Or if you got five different answers you
have to figure out which is the strongest. Of course, you
have to change all of these negative thoughts. If you are
still confused, read carefully the list I have provided and
see which one fits your life.

CHAPTER 2.

HOW DOES YOUR PERSONAL LIE OPERATE?

There are three ways your *Personal Lie* operates.

> 1. *You could act it out.*
> 2. *You could suppress it and over compensate.*
> 3. *You could project it onto others.*

You may go in and out of all three of these approaches. Let's take some examples, such as a person whose dominant lie is, "I am not good enough."

If he is doing #1, he acts not good enough and does things in a not good enough way. He may walk in the room and you might think he was not dressed well enough. Probably he wasn't.

If he is doing #2 he may suppress that thought and overcompensate by trying to be super great at everything; however, he does not really believe in himself anyway.

If he is doing #3 he will think his mate is not good enough, his job is not good enough, his boss is not good enough, his kids are not good enough etc. etc. He projects that thought onto all kinds of things outside of himself.

Let's take someone who has the personal lie, "I am bad."

If he is doing #1, he will actually do bad things and he gets in trouble a lot to prove he is bad. Sometimes he will get kind of "high" by being the bad guy.

If he is doing #2, he will suppress that and try to be goody two shoes constantly—but he will not feel good about it. Even when he is "doing good," he will feel underneath it all he is "bad."

If he is doing #3 he will see others as bad, make them wrong and or attract bad mates, bad business partners, bad situations, etc.

Let's take someone who has a personal lie "I am wrong." If she is doing #1 she will do the wrong thing, go the wrong way, or say things that are wrong. She may continually attract a partner who is wrong for her.

If she is doing #2 she will suppress that and always have a need to be right. She may become a people pleaser and attempt to make everyone feel all right, because underneath she feels so wrong all the time.

If she is doing #3 she will always think the other is wrong—and will make others wrong. Her partner is wrong. Her car is wrong, her job is wrong. Everything is "wrong."

Got the idea? When one gets really clear on his or her "Personal Lie," he or she must carefully study how it is operating in his or her life. This takes a great deal of introspection. One must be alert as to when it is coming up and actively try to change the thought on the spot.

SOME COMMON PERSONAL LIES

Personal lie = "I can't."

This person may have the thought, "I can't make it," "I can't do it," "I can't get what I want," etc.   Sometimes these people might create mysterious illnesses or diseases that cannot be diagnosed. Then they will think "I can't heal myself," or "I can't be healed." So then they go into helplessness and despair. They may get in financial situations that are not profitable, with the thought, "I can't win." They may go so far as to get stuck in, "I can't give up the thought I can't."

Personal lie = "I am a failure."
Imagine a person trying to heal him or herself of any condition, medical, emotional, financial or whatever with this thought. It won't work. They have set themselves up to fail at self-healing, relationships, and/or career. This could get so bad that their death urge comes up and they want to check out. The conditions then all get worse fast. The personal lie can be brutal!

Personal lie = "I shouldn't be here." Or, "I don't want to be here."
This is also a very tough one and can be deadly. These people naturally have quite a death urge and may even go around creating fatal accidents and illnesses. More often than not, they live on the edge of personal disaster. They go around bragging to others how many near misses with death they have had. They may have a lot of 'out of the body' experiences, and might even make good clairvoyants for that reason. These people are guilty for being alive. Their mothers may have tried to abort them. So, they think they should not be wherever they are. They may think, "I should not be here in this relationship," also. But they really don't want to be here.

Personal lie = "I am unwanted."

People with this thought pattern are often attracted to people of the opposite sex who are not attracted to them and don't want them. That way they can FEEL unwanted. The sadness of constant rejection is devastating.

But they don't really want those that want them! They often cannot ask for the help they need because they think others don't want to help them. They may even marry the first person who finally asks their hand even if they are not in love because they think nobody else will want them.

Personal lie = "Something is wrong with me."

This personal lie is a pretty obvious sure bet that something wrong will be created in the body. For example, I have known women with fertility problems that had this syndrome. They ran from doctor to doctor trying to get "proof" of infertility. It drove them nuts if the doctors found nothing wrong. What they did not see was that the infertility problem was the result of their personal lie, and actually nothing was wrong at all. I have known women with fertility problems who gave themselves up as hopeless, yet, after they had a Liberation Breathing Session and breathed out that thought, they became pregnant. Go figure!

Personal lie = "I am nothing."

These people have very low self-esteem, and they may think they deserve nothing. Often they manifest anorexia or other diseases that waste away the body. The sad part is that they almost never reach out for help for they believe that nothing exists out there to help them. They are often atheists and deny the support of God and the universe. This is a dangerous thought pattern as they can easily wipe themselves out. They could create near death experiences. They often end up thinking "Nothing works". We have even had some of these cases project on to us that we are nothing so they think we cannot help them. They feel like something if they can "transfer" their personal lie to us. Very Tricky!!

In my case, my personal lie was "I am not perfect." I felt I did not please everyone at my birth because my sister definitely wanted a brother, not a sister to compete with. She went to the window (I was born at home) and said to her friends outside. "We had a boy but it came out a girl." So I did not please her.

All my years in school I would cry if I did not get straight A's. I was trying to over—compensate. My mother said; "I don't know why you are crying, I am not insisting you make straight A's." But I was obsessed. An A minus is not perfect. So I felt not perfect.

Then when I was a basket ball star, we won 34 straight games. The final tournament we lost by 1 point. There it was again. I was not perfect. Then I would write very good books but the cover art work would always be off. So there was one thing not perfect once again. I usually also managed to find one thing off in my body. It was very helpful when I started breathwork to understand these dynamics so I could finally relax.

The reason it was so difficult for me to let go of this thought was this: if I got off it and therefore was perfect, that would be blasphemy according to my church. You cannot be perfect like God. This was brainwashed into me so strongly that I thought I would die if I committed blasphemy. So this made my case very complicated and not only did I have fear of not being perfect, I had more fear of being perfect.

So in my case I had to process myself on my fear of giving up my personal lie. That process got me to the bottom of everything which had to do with the church !

MARKUS SHARES ABOUT HIS CASE

As Sondra says, "Everyone has a case!" And when we get to the point in which we can *face our case*, and see the intricacies of how it manifests in our life, then we are ready to be free of it. It may take many sessions of

25

Liberation Breathing with a skilled Practitioner to help us *crack our case*, as we say.

I was born in Hollywood, California, in the 1950's. It was a time of great promise. My parents had moved to California from Ohio, and they already had my sister. I was very much wanted and very much planned. But as many of us know ahead of time, we have resistance to follow through with some of the soul contracts we accepted when we chose our parents and our life's lessons before we incarnate.

My *Personal Lie(s)* are centered on two thoughts: "I don't want to be here," and "I am guilty." My mother got pregnant with me, and my thought, "I don't want to be here," came up. So I miscarried. This was devastating for my mom. She felt bad and then I felt bad as a result. I felt "guilty" that I did not follow through and incarnate. So then I "came again" the second time. This time my mother was determined that I would make it. She drank Knox gelatin every day—and I was a robust, healthy baby. BIG! I was 9 lbs. 10 oz. and 24" long when I was born! Also, I was induced at birth, because my doctor wanted to go on vacation, and I was not coming out! So that made me mad, as I felt manipulated and not allowed to come out on my own.

Another factor was around my father's health. He became ill with hepatitis and could not work as a result. Therefore, after I was born my parents' financial situation deteriorated. Within the first year of my life our family moved back to Ohio to live with my maternal grandparents in Mount Vernon, the small central Ohio town where my mother and sister were born. This gave me more trauma and upset, because I had wanted to live in California. So between feeling scarcity and upheaval, I was pretty activated.

The good thing was my grandparents were a wonderful influence. My father recovered from hepatitis, and went on to lead a productive life. Mother worked for my grandfather's business, and then on to local businesses in their accounting departments. My sister and I had a regular small town home life.

I was very bright and did well in school, but my trauma from the early time in my first year of life, and the miscarriage from just before my life, snuck in to affect me. Mom was very over-protective, and this closeness was often at the expense of her closeness with my dad. They both were hard working people, but did not have the emotional tools to deal with relationship challenges. Mostly, any emotional upsets got swept under the rug. I became introverted. This caused me to shut down, and excel even more at school, which was an escape from the emotional tension in my home life. Somehow, I felt responsible for their upsets (as many children do), which reinforced my thoughts, "I am guilty," and, "I don't want to be here."

It was not until I found Rebirthing and *A Course in Miracles* in the mid 1980s that I began to face myself, and the inner workings of my *Personal Lie*. Most of us feel responsible for the shortcomings of our family life, and the struggles and tribulations that our parents go through raising us. For me this "unhappiness" was deeply felt, and I turned it into an underlying guilt that wanted things to be better, more joyous and free flowing. I would retreat into my school work or hobbies. Rather than talk a lot, I loved to do things with my hands. I painted. I played the violin. I built model trains. I played baseball in the summer. These were the things that interested me.

What really got me over my *Personal Lie*? *A Course in Miracles* says, "Forgiveness is the key to happiness." *(ACIM; Workbook; Lesson #121)* The forgiveness that I discovered from Breathwork and working with *ACIM* was what broke me through it. Also, seeing that the duality of thought will always keep us in a battle with ourselves. My teacher, Tara Singh, helped me with this point. Just to see the inherent battle of thought itself is a major realization, and a major step in removing the biggest block to Pure Joy. Also, from Sondra Ray and Rebirthing, I saw that thoughts always produce results—even our subconscious ones we do not even realize we have.

The *Personal Lie* is our biggest saboteur in life. But it is just a thought! And—we have dominion over our thoughts. Another lesson in *ACIM* says, "I rule my mind, which I alone must rule." *(ACIM; Workbook; Lesson #236)* It is up to us to change our minds. But not in the sense of trading one "good thought" for a "bad thought." It is in seeing that the subconscious mind is mostly in charge of us, and this pull toward "opposites" is the nature of it. When we step out of the very thought system that generates opposites, guilt and conflict, we are truly free. *A Course in Miracles* introduced me to my God created Mind, which is free of opposites. The easiest thing to do is to let go and surrender. But to the ego, which is embroiled in self-imposed justifications, it is the "hardest thing." The intellect will weave all kinds of reasons for keeping the *Personal Lie*—proven by experiences.

One important fact to see is that thought always precedes its experience—or manifestation. The thought "I don't want to be here" preceded my miscarriage. The thought "I am guilty" was around to attract the miscarriage, my sticky emotional ties with my mother, and feeling responsible for my parents' struggles.

Just seeing this dynamic, and choosing out of it, brings stillness and silence into our Mind. It is not possible for our *Personal Lie* to be "true,"—even though we have felt and experienced its "effects." When I realized this simple logic as a result of my association with Tara Singh, and from Rebirthing with Sondra Ray, the advent of God's Grace entered my life. I saw my inherent *innocence,* and really decided *I want to be here.*

Chapter 3.

HEALING THE ROOT CAUSE OF YOUR PROBLEMS

Sometimes you think you know your *Personal Lie* and you might not be going deep enough. Let's say you have a Liberation Breathing session with a powerful breathworker who is well trained. That breathworker will surely double check your *Personal Lie* and you might end up with a different one if you had not gone deep enough. You can usually tell if you have the right one because your body reacts and you feel like you have to take deep breaths or you might cry. You can also tell by looking at your life. This will explain in so many cases why things turned out the way they did.

Now you are finding out one of the most important things Liberation Breathing has to offer—overcoming your *Personal Lie*. Until this is discovered and released, one cannot reach full potential and you are held back. You may be doing great, but you will become a lot greater after you uncover this one. It definitely blocks your happiness and aliveness. It is the cornerstone of the ego. The ego is a collection of negative thoughts you have accumulated to prevent you from remembering you are one with God. For sure, the worst lie is "I am separate from God." (Or, "I am separate from my Source of Life.") That came first in you a long time ago. Then you go on saying, "I am not one with God, I am bad," (or whatever your particular *lie* is). So right away you are invalidating your Divinity with this lie. As I said, we call it a *lie* because God did not create you that way.

You don't overcome this overnight since it is an addiction. You don't overcome it simply by changing it to the opposite. Yes, you do need to do that (state the opposite), but at first you might not believe the new thought. Furthermore, the old *Personal Lie* is lodged in your cells. That is precisely why you need Liberation Breathing to get liberated from it. Shortly after I first started being a breathworker in 1974, my guru Babaji gave me a biology lesson in my dream. He said, "Look into this microscope and remind yourself what a healthy cell looks like." So I did. Then he said, "Now, look in this other microscope and look how the cell is damaged by one's personal lie." So I did. It was eroded. So now you see why the breathing is important as it fills up the cells, like one is blowing up a balloon. The breath pushes out the negative matter and heals the cells.

Some of the *Personal Lies* are taken up during ones birth trauma. "I am unwanted," would be from one's conception trauma. "I am a disappointment," might be taken up when one realizes they are not the sex their parents wanted. Others are very obviously coming from past lives: such as, "I am evil," and, "I am a killer." It is not so important to know when you got stuck on this. It is important to know that it has been a long time you have had that thought. With that thought you create situations that prove it to be *right*, and then it gets more stuck. You will unconsciously set up these situations.

For example, if one has a *Personal Lie*, "I am guilty", he will unconsciously do or say inappropriate things that make him feel really guilty. Then he will believe the thought even more. The only way out of this trap is to transcend this thought with God's Divine Help. Simply saying, "I am innocent," a few times will not do the trick. You likely won't believe this new thought since you are so used to believing that your personal lie is true. So you have to reprogram and reprogram with the opposite thought in the form of an affirmation. You have to accept in yourself that the new affirmation is the real truth. Then you must add Energy to this new thought with the breathing component.

You will likely encounter resistance to giving up your *Personal Lie* completely, because your whole life has been about proving it, wrestling with it, and working around it one way or another. Some people are also very afraid of change. They would rather hang onto what is familiar rather than go through a mini-death of their old self. Sometimes we are also afraid of change because our actual birth was a huge change (from liquid to air) and we got hurt going through that process.

Some people fear the tremendous increase in energy they would get by letting it go. This is another reason to stick with Liberation Breathing sessions. After each session you experience a big increase in energy—and if you keep on this spiritual path you will adjust to increased energy.

Some people even think they will die if they give up their *Personal Lie.* In other words, they formed it at their birth and they survived their birth so they think it is part of their "survival script" or formula. This however is just a trick of the ego.

Some people have a fear of being "free" (Liberated), as they would then be in their power. People often have fear of being in their power because they misused their power in past lives and the consequences were bad.

Aren't you tired of being held back? I can assure you that your life will be so much better without that thought. It will be like Heaven without it. But ask for God's help to give it up. Markus and I were in London one night in our hotel asking how we could help people give up this addiction faster. It took years of working on ourselves to get beyond it and even still it would rear its ugly head. So, we finally came up with these 8 steps you need to do.

THE PERSONAL LIE UNDO-REDO PROCESS

1. I forgive myself for thinking (put your *Personal Lie* here).
2. God did not create me (like that).
3. The truth about me is that (put the opposite of your *Personal Lie* here).
4. I am as God created me.
5. Therefore, that thought is a lie.
6. I give up my stubborn refusal to let it go.
7. I turn this whole matter over to the Holy Spirit.
8. I am willing to see myself as (opposite of your *Personal Lie*, which is your *Eternal Truth*).

Write all that out and keep writing it out until you "get it!" Shout it from the rooftops! Here is an example of this

Undo-Redo Process using the *Personal Lie*, "I am not enough."

1. I forgive myself for ever thinking I am not enough.
2. God did not create me not enough.
3. The truth about me is that I am enough.
4. I am as God created me.
5. Therefore, that thought, "I am not enough," is a lie.
6. I give up my stubborn refusal to let it go.
7. I turn this whole matter over to the Holy Spirit.
8. I am willing to see myself as totally enough.

Even just today a student contacted me all upset and ill over the fact that she had lent a lot of her inheritance to a friend and the friend was not paying her back. When I processed her to see why she did this she said, "I wanted to feel loved and I wanted to feel enough." Her two most negative thoughts were, "I am not lovable," and, "I am not enough." So, her *Personal Lie(s)* tricked her again.

Just recently we had a client whose personal lie was, "I am weak." This thought caused her to stay in a verbally abusive relationship—as she was "too weak" to get out of it! Then after a few breathwork sessions she got the courage to go for a divorce. But she let this husband keep on living in the house because she was "too weak" to ask him to leave. She is still working out this thought and we are helping her; but as I said, it takes some time.

Recently we had a client who was an alcoholic and he wanted to stop drinking. His personal lie was, "I am a disappointment." He felt he was disappointing everyone in his family and friends by not being able to stop drinking. We tried to point out to him that the thought came first. He was drinking so he could prove the thought, "I am a disappointment."

He created the session being a disappointment because he could not stay awake to breathe. He was tired because he did not sleep much the night before. I was disappointed in his breathing and also by the fact we could not do any follow up since he left for his home country the next day. Hopefully the affirmations that Markus wrote him will help him some. It never is enough to have just one session. People need to commit to at least ten sessions.

There is a principle discussed in *A Course in Miracles* that talks about the nature of the ego. The ego seeks solutions to problems but always makes sure it never really solves them. The "tendency" of the ego is to "seek but not find." We love to seek, but when the solution is put in front of us, too often we go into evasion or denial. The ego is inherently unwilling to be liberated. It loves its misery in some ways, although it says it wants to be free of it. Something that is familiar is more in our comfort zone, even if it is painful and problematic, because the solution takes us into a place of the Unknown.

Chapter 4.

DOVETAILING PERSONAL LIES

We have to understand that Life is a relationship, and in relationships our positive aspects enhance our happiness, but our negative tendencies debilitate us. There is such a thing as two *Personal Lies* "relating." We call this phenomena "Dovetailing Personal Lies."

It is very important not only for you to understand how you are playing with your *Personal Lie*; but it is equally important to understand the *Personal Lie* of your partner. I will give you a strong example from some students of mine.

The wife's personal lie was, "I am wrong," as she was the wrong sex at birth. Her parents wanted a boy. Her husband's personal lie was, "I am bad," because he was a cesarean and really hurt his mother a lot at his birth. So then, "I am wrong," married, "I am bad." (Get it?) In the marriage he was always telling her, "You are wrong," (which was her thought about herself). Then she would feel guilty. Guilt demands punishment so he would verbally abuse her as a punishment. Then he would feel he was bad (which was his thought about himself).

One day he actually hit her. Then she felt really wrong and he felt really bad. This escalated. I came into the situation in time to get her out of an abusive marriage. But I told her, "If you don't change your thought, you will just re-create the same scenario in the next relationship." I lost track of her. She disappeared from my life for four years. Then one day there was a knock on my door and it was her. She said to me, "Four years ago, you told me what my case was but I did not get it. Then I went to India and it all came up. I promised Babaji I would give up all my addictions; but I saw my worst addiction below them all was my addiction to the thought, 'I am wrong.' "

She taught me that the *Personal Lie* is actually an addiction. It is even a physical addiction, as the memories of this negative thought are stored in the physicality of our cells. We will discuss later on the way we process addictions, but first here are some more examples of Dovetailing *Personal Lies.*

We worked with another couple who had the following personal lies. Hers was, "I am not wanted." His was, "I am not capable." She was desperate to have a baby right away as that was going to make her feel really wanted by him. He did not feel capable of handling that. They fought a lot about this. Another way her personal lie was operating was he did not WANT what she wanted (which was a baby). That made her feel more unwanted. The more she pressured him the more incapable he felt. He needed more time. He was a methodical type of person, who needed a clear structure of security in order to fell capable. "Winging it" did not cut it for him. He needed to plan in advance. We had to give them both several sessions plus consultations. We were able to get her to slow down and help her to see he wanted her even though he needed more time. He then felt more capable of handling the situation. They did get married and are doing well. Last we heard she is pregnant now. When they understood how their "cases" were dovetailing together, they were more able to ease up and support one another through their patterns.

Another couple we worked with had a huge problem because the guy started having affairs. Her case was, "I am not wanted," so you can see how she attracted that because she always felt unwanted whenever he would have an affair. His personal lie was, "I am a secret." This was because his parents got pregnant with him in high school and he was conceived in the back of the car at an outdoor movie. His parents tried to hide the pregnancy. Turns out his father was also fantasizing about other women when he was conceived. This made him always want other women. It has taken them years to let go of this addiction but it is finally working out. He has overcome this addiction. She broke up with him numerous times, but she waited for him because she could not be in love with anyone else. So now they are getting back together. He is more forthright, no longer a "secret," and she is more clear that she is truly wanted.

Here is a very interesting case . The husband told us he had a many year history of problems with erection. He had tried everything to solve this. He had had a wonderful childhood with no abuse. He was a very positive thinker and was a beautiful soul. Our hearts really went out to him. The other problem he faced was that his wife was verbally abusing him. When we saw the wife she admitted that, and asked for help with her rage. I don't know if anyone else could have helped the—were it not for understanding their *Personal Lies.* The cause of his erection problem was definitely his *Personal Lie*, "I am weak." He also felt weak around his wife's verbal abuse. The reason she attracted a "weak" man was because her father was abusive and she did not want to marry an abusive man so she chose a really nice guy who was "weak." Her *Personal Lie* was, "I am bad." That is why she incarnated into an abusive family. She thought she deserved only that because she was "bad," due to her past lives. She would then abuse her husband (stuck in her father's mind), and then she would feel "bad," which was her thought about herself. She would feel "bad" about being mean to her husband, and then he would feel "weak," as a result of being verbally abused. They were actually a great couple in their higher selves. They were really willing to take our advice and the wife even decided she should come to India with us.

They had a total shift once they saw the dynamics of their worst thoughts about themselves playing out, and applied the affirmations of forgiveness, and each took 100% responsibility for creating these results. Breathwork also helped them to let go. It's like they are in a new marriage now. They reconceived the whole thing!

Sometimes a couple ends up with the same *Personal Lie*. One client we had was a man, but was wanted as a girl at birth. So his *Personal Lie* was "I am not good enough as a man," or, "I am not wanted as a man." He over-compensated for this by having very intense high energy—where he almost seemed manic to be good enough. His communication therefore became rough. His girlfriend was wanted as a boy so her personal lie was, "I am not wanted as a girl." Her father was very disappointed in her being a girl instead of a boy so she felt guilty and attracted verbal abuse from her father. In her relationships she attracted verbal abuse. This relationship was the second one like that. He would *raise the energy* in his communication to feel good enough, but as a result his communication would come across as rough and abusive. Then she did not want him, and then he felt unwanted as a man by her. They would break off and get back together a lot. They ended up pushing each other away all the time so they could both feel unwanted.

Explaining this dynamic to them was very helpful as they were not aware of it. We got the man to tone his energy down and study types of verbal abuse we mentioned in the Loving Relationship Training. He put that list up on the wall and really looked at how his communication was too much in its emphatic nature. And he started to change it.

We had to give him affirmations like:

- My communication is gentle.
- I am good enough to be loved and wanted as a man.
- I am good enough to have good communication.
- I forgive Mother for wanting a girl.
- Anger and bad communication no longer exist in my reality.

For the woman in this case:

- It is safe to be wanted as a girl.
- God wants me to be a woman.
- I forgive all men who have been abusive, especially my father.
- I intuitively know how to be a woman.

One couple had a long-distance relationship and lived in two different countries. The gal's personal lie was. "I am disconnected," so she could never quite get connected with her man to live in the same country. His personal lie was, "I am not enough." He attracted unbalanced women because he wanted to save them, to prove that he is enough. In this case he created a relationship in which they did not spend enough time together, so he could feel the relationship was "not enough."

In another couple, her personal lie was, "I do not want to be here." As a consequence, she had no joy in her life. She was with a guy who was working a lot to support the family. His personal lie was, "I am guilty." They had not had sex for years. But they had a child and wanted to stay together. The way their personal lies dovetailed was this, he was guilty for having had inappropriate sexual energy with relatives in his childhood. He was therefore putting up a wall with his guilt—and so she was turned off to sex with him. This did not contribute to any joy in their marriage so she wanted to be here even less. It was like, "I don't want to be here in this relationship."

It is important to realize this point: The *Personal Lie* precedes the manifestation of things not working out in life. Not the other way around. Thought always comes before manifestation. In the case of the woman who "did not want to be here," that thought was lodged in her memory long before she manifested a marriage in which she did not want to be here. In the case of the man whose *Personal Lie* was, "I am guilty," that thought came before his attraction to inappropriate sexual energy with family members. Experiences are just a confirmation of the vibrational match to the underlying thoughts and beliefs that attract those experiences.

I think from these examples of *Personal Lies* Dovetailing, you get the importance of unravelling these main negative thoughts that cause a lot of suffering in relationships. Now the question is, how do we free ourselves from them, and restore harmony and happiness to our Self and Relationships?

Chapter 5.

THE NATURE OF THOUGHT ITSELF

By Markus

It would be helpful to look at the nature of thought itself. What is it exactly? It is an energy, a vibration. For the most part, in the relative world of what we can observe, thought manifests a form. It can manifest things, and the relationships between things. It can describe or harness the energy of opposites. We live in a world of opposites. This is the nature of relative thought: Up vs. Down; Good vs. Evil; White vs. Black; Light vs. Dark; Stillness vs Movement; Happy vs. Sad; Love vs. Hate; Truth vs. Lies.

Is there such a thing as an Absolute Thought System which is totally Liberated from opposites?

Can we consider an Absolute Thought System in which there are no "opposites?" A Truth is always true in this system. The Absolute Truth is that thoughts always produce some result. A thought always produces a similar vibrational result, match, or manifestation. This is a true statement. We could call it a Law. Because it is a Law, it is always true, and therefore does not have an opposite. It is an Absolute Thought.

The problem is we live most of the time in a state of relative thought. Thoughts and their results fluctuate, and sometimes we find ourselves in a state of well-being, and sometimes we find ourselves in stress and duress. Our existence seems wracked with opposites. Therefore, it is perennially uncertain, in conflict—either actually or potentially in conflict.

We base our actions in life on what we know, and within this "known" of relative thought, there are conflicts and *Personal Lies*.

The *Personal Lie* is a mainstay in this relative thought system. The problem with it is we think it is "true." We think a "lie" about ourselves is "true," and we confirm that it is when we actually feel it's "effects." We cite our experiences to *prove it*. But the *cause* always precedes its *effects*. We are responsible for the cause, therefore we have control over its effects—its *feelings*. The problem is we feel the effects of the "lie" more than we feel the effects of the truth—so we evade correcting the cause and liberating ourselves from our "lie."

If our *Personal Lie* is, "I am not enough," then we live in the feeling of this scarcity—even in the midst of an Absolutely Abundant Universe. Until we see we are causing our own sense of lack, and trade in our relative thought system of the ego for the Absolute Thought System of our Higher Self, we may still be subject to the appearances of the *Personal Lie*—and *its effects.*

What does it take to step out of relative thought for the Silence and the Stillness of Absolute Thought?

The first step, like in seeing the fact that the *Personal Lie* has been running our life, is to see that we have been caught in the fluctuation and uncertainty of relative thought most of our life. It's no wonder we have political strife, personal strife, family strife, in a world in which the nature of thought itself is conflict and strife.

We study *A Course in Miracles* which makes the two thought systems very clear. The Absolute Thought System of our Source of Life—called God—is what can Liberate us from the conflicts of the relative thought system of the ego, which is run by our *Personal Lies.*

"My thoughts do not mean anything," *(ACIM; Workbook; Lesson #10)* because they are not permanent and True. It is true that they result in the appearances and experiences of all the temporal ups and downs in our world. But these highs and lows are of our own making. Only the permanence of Love, Peace and Joy—in their Absolute state—is True. This permanent, Absolute, never changing Reality, is something with which I can and must make contact within myself. The whole meaning of Liberation lies in this shift out of the relative thought system of "conflict" into the Absolute Thought System of Love, Peace and Joy.

In fact, "There is no Peace except the Peace of God," *(ACIM; Workbook; Lesson #200)* or, this Absolute state. Peace, by its very nature, is that which has no conflict. It has no opposite called "war." The relative thought system of the ego is full of conflict; therefore, "relative peace" has no meaning.

I was born on Armistice Day, November 11th, which in 1918 was the day to commemorate the end of World War I. They called it the day to mark a peace that was, "the end of all wars." Well, we know that was relative, therefore not really true. That *peace* easily turned to *war*—seven times more destructive than before—just a couple of decades later in World War II.

In the realm of relative thought, the seeds of peace can grow into the fruits of war, also. We all can easily see this. To be free of our *Personal Lies*, we have to see this dilemma of thought itself. It requires that we transcend the relative nature of thought, and ascend into the more orderly realms of Absolute thoughts of God—of the Life Source—which are not touched by opposites.

In this System of Reality, only what is True is true. It does not have an opposite. And what is a "lie," or rather, what is false about us, does not exist. It is not a truth, even if we have been "acting it out" most of our life and producing "effects" to "prove" it to ourselves.

Chapter 6.

OVERCOMING YOUR WORST ADDICTION

By Sondra

As I mentioned above, one of my students had a personal lie, "I am wrong," and after her whole marriage unravelled, I lost track of her. She went to India, to the feet of our Master Babaji, to get some real answers. What she heard was startling. The *Personal Lie* is our worst addiction. She discovered her biggest addiction was to the thought, "I am wrong."

Overcoming addictions is not easy, as most of us know. In our work, we get people to look at their fear of giving up the addiction. There would be a fear, or you would already have given it up. Usually there is a neurotic benefit you are getting from keeping the addiction—you

get attention, you get to remain helpless, you don't have to take responsibility, you get to stay hidden and small, you don't have to face the world—those sorts of reasons.
In order to let go of the Personal Lie, we also have to let go of our "payoffs" for keeping it. There is some kind of benefit we are getting from keeping it.

So first we ask people to say to themselves: "My fear of giving up the thought, (your personal lie), is _____."
You would be surprised what people say. Sometimes they will say, "I would die." In other words, they can only conceive of themselves with the limiting belief. Sometimes it would be, "I would be killed," which could be a memory from a past life in which they were killed for being in too much of their own personal power—such as by the Church or ruling authorities.

Another common fear, close to mine is, "I would be perfect, and that is 'blasphemy' to think I am perfect. Only God is perfect."

For people with a *Personal Lie,* "I am not enough," the fear could be, "I would be abundant and powerful, and I would have to be too responsible. I would be overwhelmed by people's demands on me."

For someone with a *Personal Lie*, "I am bad," we have heard this fear: "People would try to sabotage me." Their benefit is to keep themselves out of the limelight with the thought, "I am bad," so they are not subject to other's criticism. They are their own "worst critics," before they get subjected to the scrutiny of others.

The other way you can pull out your fear of giving up your *Personal Lie* is to approach it from its positive side. For the thought "I am not wanted," you could phrase the question like this: "My fear of being wanted all the time is _____." What? Some people with this thought might respond, "I would be trapped, or smothered." They cannot envision being wanted without being controlled or held hostage. In other words, they feel more freedom by maintaining the thought of not being wanted. It's kind of a self-imposed exile from true happiness.

The *Personal Lie* is very tricky. It will keep you working on the wrong piece of your case to remain hidden. Sometimes people will work on a very superficial negative thought, like, "I am not good enough," when really underneath is a thought, "I am worthless." The real *Personal Lie* may be too painful to face.

Someone may be working to overcome the thought, "I am not enough," but underneath that they really have a thought, "I am a complete failure." So you see, it is important to keep asking yourself if you are going deep enough, and does the *Personal Lie* you have uncovered really explain your life? Does it apply to how you felt in situations in your life that were traumatic or did not go well for you?

Because these negative thoughts are addictions, you have to be vigilant to see how they are persistently infiltrating your experiences. You know you are over your *Personal Lie* when you no longer see its results cropping up in your life. This may take some time. One of the main ways you overcome this negative thought is through forgiveness. So if the thought is still manifesting, more forgiveness is needed, not more judgments that you have not yet got over it! You may have had this thought for 50 lifetimes unaware of it, and now you finally are facing it. Give yourself a break. Be gentle with yourself in your process. To heal the subconscious mind of its deep-seeded patterning, we have to be patient, forgiving, gentle, and loving.

THE FORGIVENESS DIET

I have mentioned this in my book, *The Only Diet There Is*. It would be good to mention it here, now we are on the subject of forgiveness. All forgiveness is of our self. Even when others my seem to be the culprit of our woes, it is we who attract their behaviour toward us with our negative thoughts and feelings, and yes—our *Personal Lie*. ACIM says, "Forgiveness is the key to happiness," and "Forgiveness offers everything I want." *(ACIM;*

Workbook; Lessons #121 & #122) Forgiveness of a true nature is the most important tool in our repertoire to overcome our *worst addiction.*

When I was working with a group of clients who had an overweight issue, I tried this experiment. I asked them what was the thought that was keeping them from letting go of the extra weight. Most of them expressed some kind of anger towards their fathers, who had either been angry, or critical, or emotionally absent, or something. So I had them all do what I called at the time, "The Forgiveness Diet."

I got the idea from Jesus in the Bible when He was asked how many times one should forgive another for the same infraction. He said, "Forgive them seventy times seven." (Which is 490 times, which later I discovered in Numerology means completion.) So I had the gals write, "I forgive my Father completely," 70 X's a day for 7 Days. In long hand. The miraculous thing was that they all lost weight, without changing their eating habits. It had nothing to do with the food at all. It had everything to do with the unresolved and "heavy" emotions they harboured toward their fathers. When they let go of those grievances, they lost the weight automatically. When they released the past, they were free of the fear and negative thoughts which contributed to hanging on to the weight.

Forgiveness, when done properly by taking 100% responsibility, without any blame, is truly the "key to happiness." It releases you from the addictive thoughts from the past, and puts you in the Grace of the Present. It dissolves your *Personal Lie*, and puts you in your Eternal Truth. It is the ultimate Liberation.

You can do *The Forgiveness Diet* on Yourself first, and then anyone else with whom you still may have *a charge*. If you find yourself falling back into old patterns of judgments, you can do it again. The main thing here is that you make forgiveness a way of life, and taking responsibility for your thoughts a kind of "detective work" that keeps your mind clear. When something goes off in your life, you can easily ask, "What is the thought in me that caused this situation?" Usually, it has something to do with your *Personal Lie*, if not a direct manifestation of it. Forgive yourself. Change your thoughts for an Absolute one, and move on. Pick yourself up, and walk forward into a brighter day.

CHAPTER 7.

WHAT IS PURE JOY?

By Markus

"We hold these truths to be self-evident." The Declaration of Independence guarantees us the right to "life, liberty and the pursuit of happiness." Pursuit, in this case, means more like the "practice of" rather than the "chasing of" happiness. Happiness is a kind of *unalienable right*. Though the implication is that a government should safeguard and protect our right to practice a broad "pursuit of happiness," it leaves it up to us the "how and wherefore" of this pursuit.

Happiness. What is that for you?

People pursue this in many ways, in different stages of their life. What is the Happiness that has no opposite?

What is the Joy that never reverts back to sadness? Is there a Pure Joy that does not rely on external conditions or achievements in order to be ours? A *Course in Miracles* has this to say about Pure Joy:

> "There is one thought in particular that should be remembered throughout the day. It is a thought of *pure joy*, a thought of peace, a thought of limitless release, limitless because all things are freed within it." (ACIM; Teacher's Manual; 16.; ¶6)

Pure Joy is a thought, liberated, *freed* from your *Personal Lie*. It is an awareness of happiness, of "limitless release." It is a thought of Absolute, and complete freedom. It is Liberation. It is Freedom. Liberation is Pure Joy.

There is also a lesson that speaks of a higher Will, which also brings clarity to Pure Joy:

> *"God's Will for me is perfect happiness."* (ACIM; Workbook; Lesson #101)

The Divine Creator is a Will, and this Will for me is Perfect Happiness, or in other words, Pure Joy. If the entire Will of the Life Force of the Cosmos is for me to experience and maintain Perfect Happiness, would I not want to focus my attentions on that? What better focus should I have for my life?

The *Personal Lie* is mutually exclusive of Pure Joy. Therefore, it does not inhabit the Absolute Thought System of Divine Reality. How can I maintain a thought of Perfect Happiness and the thought, "I am not good enough," at the same time? It is obvious each deny the other. Pure Joy is Liberation from thoughts of limitations and conflicts; from judgments and condemnations. Pure Joy is an embrace of our natural innocence, free of the dogmatic notions of religious *original sin*. We may have made a mistake thinking our *Personal Lie*, but all mistakes can be corrected (without punishment).

Pure Joy is an acceptance of our Self as God created us.

In silence, and stillness, no explanation of Who we really are is needed. In the blessing of Pure Joy, there is nothing to achieve, nothing to get, nothing yet to gain. We already are in possession of Pure Joy—why would we not want to awaken it?

Liberation is freeing ourselves from everything that would stand in the way of us being in a state of Pure Joy. Freedom from our biggest block to Pure Joy is Liberation from our *Personal Lie*, which is also the main purpose of Liberation Breathing.

Ultimately this is a matter of Self-Identity. We relinquish the self we made up, fragmented and stuck in a quagmire of conflicts, measurements, judgments, and duality—for an awakening of the Self God created—which is unified and whole, Absolute and certain of our Divine Inheritance of Pure Joy.

This shift is the only real purpose of Yoga and all Spiritual Practices. The *pursuit of happiness* is nothing short of this total Liberation—freedom from the *Personal Lie*.

Chapter 8.

Liberation

Freedom. Liberty. Unencumbered Well Being. Divine Aloofness. Dignity. Independence. Self-Reliance. All these compose the qualities of Liberation. And also lead us to a Life free of problems.

There are other qualities that accompany Liberation. Grace. Mercy. Benevolence. Care & Safety.

This little book is called **Liberation** mainly because it is directed toward liberating you from your *Personal Lie*, your biggest block to Pure Joy. Also, Liberation is a necessity—from darkness into light—from the conflicts that are inherent in a relative thought system of *Personal Lies*—to the Absolute Thought System of Pure Joy. In this Reality, the Eternal Law of your True Self is free of all limitations. It has no "lies" in it to reconcile. It is connected to the Will of Perfect Happiness. This is its function. This is your purpose for living. To be an expression of Pure Joy.

The seers, oracles, and sages have said over time:
"KNOW THYSELF."

Who is this Self of Pure Joy? Have we realized it yet? This little booklet is designed to remove one of the biggest blocks people have to this Self-Realization—the *Personal Lie*. I think we have defined it pretty well, shown you how it operates, and helped you with some tools you can use to Liberate yourself from it.

Liberation is a kind of "Heaven on Earth." Contrary to a utopian pipe-dream conjured up in the ivory towers of intellectual speculations, the Heaven we speak of is a decision we make. It is a very real and demonstrable decision we can make right now, and does not need conditions to be altered or changed to be conducive for some forthcoming Nirvana. Heaven is Now inside of you. It is a transcendence over your lower relative self, to your Higher Absolute Self. It is a Liberation from your *Personal Lie* to the Eternal Truth of Pure Joy within you.

Liberation is more of a subtraction than an addition. Your God-Created-Self is already perfect, and the self you made up to cover it over is all that needs to be removed to restore your perfection. This is the first and last step anyone needs to take on the journey to enlightenment. The *Personal Lie*, a major component of the self you made up, is the main thing to remove. This is the main thing from which everyone needs Liberation.

THE USE OF THE BREATH FOR LIBERATION

Thoughts and memories are stored not only in the brain, but also in every cell. Bruce Lipton, Ph.D., wrote a whole book on this, called *The Biology of Belief*. This is why a physical cleansing of the *Personal Lie* is not only helpful, but considered necessary. Rebirthing was discovered in 1974 by many of us who were taught by Leonard Orr, it's founder. And we have since understood this circular, conscious connected Energy Breathing is the best way to help clear ourselves of thoughts and memories on the cellular level, including our *Personal Lie*. The cells are "inflated," expanded by the super infusion of Prana, which is more than just "oxygen" or "air." And in this expansion, they are cleansed of negative memory. They become more orderly and joyous. As a result, your life gets more orderly and joyous.

Liberation Breathing® is the Rebirthing process we have always used, but joined with the added Power of invoking the Divine Mother Energy as well to aid in the forgiveness and release of negative thoughts. This Power transcends our conscious control, and touches on the Unknown Forces that are beyond our manipulation. At some point, after looking at all the conscious parts of our case in need of healing, we ask a higher Power to intervene on our behalf to help release our subconscious that also needs healing. This *surrender* to the *Unknown* is necessary for the most broad and complete release. Otherwise, the limits of our thought, which made the *Personal Lie* in the first place, can sabotage our healing and maintain the very illusion we are trying to escape. Suspension into a state of mind that is Silent, transcendent of *opposites*, is a necessary part of Liberation. Liberation Breathing can help us do this.

Surrender and Liberation are very similar. We have to admit at some point our helplessness—the fact that our known world has limitations, and to escape it, or transcend it, we need the help of a Power that is bigger than us. We need the help of the Unknown. Surrender does not mean, though, that there is no work to do. We still take responsibility for the part of our minds that we know is the culprit of our woes. We still have to identify our *Personal Lie*, and own the degree it has been running us. But then what? This is exactly where surrender is needed.

The good thing about breathing is that it is both involuntary (it will go on when you are sleeping and unaware of it), and it is voluntary (you can control it with your conscious mind). Liberation Breathing is a deep, connected circular breathing, with no holding at the top of the inhale, and no pause at the bottom of the exhale. It is a smooth in and out of the breath, without too much control on the part of the breather. One gets the deep flow going, and like a flywheel of rhythmic motion, then let's go to allow the breath to continue in its own rhythmic, circular flow.

The mechanics of Liberation Breathing are not hard to learn. They could be mastered in 5 minutes. Yet, the challenge is all that comes up in one's mind and emotions as a result of doing this breathing. This is where a skilled Breathworker, or Liberation Breathing Practitioner is needed. They can help you process what comes up—very important. Also, the super infusion of more Life Force in your body as a result of this breathing can make you feel energized in a way you are not used to. If you resist this Energy, you can experience a cramping, or retraction in the muscles in the hands and feet. It is only temporary, and as you breathe and identify the "thoughts causing the stuckness," the paralysis dissipates and eventually leaves. But you need an experienced Breathworker to get you through this possible stage of tetany, as we call it.

Plus, you need someone skilled at helping you look at your thoughts and beliefs. You need to regress all the way back to your conception and birth to find the root causes of your *Personal Lie*. And sometimes this negative thought is brought in from past lives. A skilled Breathworker is used to looking at these dynamics, and can help you look at them too, and come up with new thoughts—affirmations—that free you from your negative past thoughts and beliefs. This support is essential to identify, observe the workings, and let go of the stubborn *Personal Lie*.

This book is a start, but we recommend a sustained commitment to some form of breathwork that will help you move though the thoughts and beliefs that have been affecting your life in a way you don't want. You have to get moving in a direction that will produce the Life you do want. This is where a Breathwork professional comes in. We recommend a Certified Liberation Breathing® Practitioner, because we have trained them to be not only good breath coaches, but also good at processing people's *Personal Lies*, and helping people to be Liberated from them. We are also available for private sessions booked here **bit.ly/LBSession** on our website.

THE ULTIMATE LIBERATION

Your biggest block to experiencing Pure Joy, or Heaven on Earth, is your *Personal Lie*. We made this clear in Chapter 1, and listed over 350 of them. A few of them are most likely affecting you. Especially one of them, that is your dominant negative thought about yourself. The ultimate Liberation is from your *Personal Lie*, and all of its negative effects.

You have to see as well, how is it operating in your life? Are you acting it out? Are you over-compensating for it? Are you projecting it onto others? It is good to understand the *Personal Lie's* actual effects in your life. See how it operates. Notice how it makes you feel. Notice how you feel without it.

Once you have seen its dynamics, apply the "Undo-Redo Process" to overcoming it. This is not hard, but you have to be willing to face it and allow a higher Power to help you release it. You have been stubbornly holding on to this thought like an addiction. And, in a relationship, your *Personal Lie* is meshing—or *Dovetailing*—with your mate's *Personal Lie*. It is helpful to look at this dynamic too. Shine the light of a forgiving vision onto the effects of this limitation you have imposed on yourself and on your relationships. And remember, it only is *real* in the world of relative thought. In the realm of Absolute Thought of your Self-Identity, it has no real effects. It is a *lie*, an illusion. A mirage is an illusion of something that is not really there, even though it seems like it is. Your *Personal Lie*, like a mirage, disappears with the right perspective.

The right perspective is that God's Will for you is Pure Joy. You are not meant to suffer at the effects of your *Personal Lie*. You are not meant to be a victim of any negative belief. Esther Hicks says, "A belief is just a thought you keep on thinking." It seems rigid and untransmutable only because of your habit of thinking it. So, when you are willing to think a different thought, to see things differently, the belief can be dissolved, and you are free.

LIBERATION IS FREEDOM FROM YOUR WORST BELIEF—YOUR PERSONAL LIE.

Overcoming your worst belief, one that has been an addiction, requires radical forgiveness. If I am overweight because I overate, and I overate to stuff the feeling of my personal lie, "I am guilty," or "I am not good enough," then I must be willing to look at this thought and forgive myself for thinking it. Now, I might still be overweight while in this process, but forgiveness has to come first. We have to accept the "lesson God would have us learn," and be willing to forgive and accept ourselves whether we are overweight or not. My overweightness cannot leave until I accept my innocence, and have gratitude for discovering its "cause"—my *Personal Lie*.

This would apply to any problem in your life. Usually at the bottom of it is your *Personal Lie*. When you uncover this principle cause of your problem, you may still be enmeshed in the results brought about by this negative thought. But you have got to the root of the weed, so to speak, so the weeds will not keep growing. But you may have to clean up your garden for awhile, from the weeds that have already grown up as a result of your *Personal Lie.*

Students often ask, *"Is it possible to get over my Personal Lie in this lifetime?"* We usually reply, *"Yes, but not without the help of God!"* People need to have a relationship with the greater Forces of Life. They have to invoke their Source in this matter. Some tools we developed help—the Undo-Redo Process especially to get over unwillingness and stubbornness. And The Forgiveness Diet is useful to let go of grievances that feed the *Personal Lies.* Perhaps these grievances have been held over something that happened to you many years ago. You are holding onto the hurt that is no longer even here! You can get over the *Personal Lie* with the determination to forgive and let go.

Just remember, Pure Joy is your natural state of being. You were created in this Heavenly State, and you are destined to return to it. All the bumps and bruises along the way (even over many lifetimes) are merely "lessons" of release that you have needed to learn, so don't beat yourself up for any mistakes. We have a saying when we make a mistake: *"Even though I made a mistake, I still completely love and accept myself."* The instant you notice a mistake, resulting most likely from your *Personal Lie*, correct it and return to your innocence immediately. Pure Joy is Innocence. And this is your Absolute Reality.

Liberation is then the return to Pure Joy, and freedom from your *Personal Lie*, your biggest block to Pure Joy. We have laid out the steps in this book to overcome it. We have also given you a look at what Breathwork can do in this process of inner awakening and healing. We hope you can *be all you can be*, having taken a good look at this major saboteur to Pure Joy, and *take the steps to let it go*. It is our Pure Joy to help you in this release. We thank you for reading this and taking an action on behalf of your own freedom—for the purpose of your total Liberation in this Lifetime.

LOVE,   *Sondra Ray*

&

Markus Ray

Chapter 9.

What Other Breathworkers Say about the Personal Lie

SILKE MODERSOHN IN SPAIN:

When I did my Rebirther training it was the first time I heard the word *Personal Lie*. Doing the process of, "My most negative thought I have about myself is_____," I discovered that my *Personal Lie* was, "I am not wanted."

When my parents conceived me, they were lovers. My father was Hungarian and married. He was travelling a lot, so he knew my mother in Germany, where he used to work. They had an affair and the day my mother intended to finish the relationship, she got pregnant. My father asked my mother to abort, and my mother accepted. She took a hot bath, jumped from the table and finally took some medicine to abort me. It did not work.

Because I had a strong desire to live, I stayed. But, of course, I was born with the feeling that I was not wanted. I was always very angry toward my father and felt I was a burden to my mother. Nevertheless, I only became aware of all this when I started doing Liberation Breathing. Before, I never thought about it. I was just reacting to and acting out my *Personal Lie*.

As a consequence of my birth story, I always chose men and situations where I felt not wanted, and I always had the feeling that I had to convince them to love me. My way of choosing partners was to go for a man who was showing interest, where I felt wanted. It was not about "if I wanted him." I wanted a man "who wanted me." After sometime my *Personal Lie* would get activated and I would feel not loved and rejected.

When I met the man who later would be my husband and father of my three wonderful children, he wanted to create a family and make a living by organic farming. I was not into that at all at that time. He wanted me. So, I followed him. I got pregnant and we married. Situations occurred where I started to feel not loved and rejected. This situation continued for about 16 years. You can imagine what a marriage that was. I was very unhappy. When I finally got divorced, the year later I had a relationship with a married man. For the first time I felt completely wanted and so desired. And, of course, I was repeating my parents' relationship.

After some time, this relationship started to be really painful. I was not always wanted. When he was with his wife, I felt not wanted and rejected. So, there I had the perfect scenario again. When suffering got very hard on me, Breathwork came into my life.

I started to become conscious about my patterns and my past. Using conscious breathing and releasing my *Personal Lie* was my liberation – *Liberation Breathing*. So doing the *Personal Lie* process and working on it, I could finally let go of that toxic relationship and create relationships where I felt loved and wanted.

As Rebirthing has changed my life completely, I became aware that it was my mission in life to pass on this powerful, simple and miraculous tool on to others. In my Breathwork Centre, called Pura Vida, on Tenerife in the Canary Islands, I give sessions, workshops and Liberation Breathing trainings to support others to free their lives. Working on the *Personal Lie* is a basic part of it.

Many times I have these strong looking, all muscle men, coming to have Liberation Breathing Sessions with me. Usually, it comes out that their *Personal Lie* is, "I am weak." Of course, they have to prove that they are not weak. So they go to the gym or do other sports to get muscles and show the world that they are not weak. This goes along with a lot of stress and effort, and does not really solve the problem. They are just over-compensating for a thought still running them. Sooner or later they face the fact that their life is not working and that they have a problem.

Or, these beautiful, fashionable and slim women enter my Centre looking for support. Normally their personal lie is, "I am ugly." They try by all means to be *beauties*, but if you tell them how beautiful they are, they will not believe you—because they themselves don´t believe it.

And then there are also people who do not over compensate, but just assume their *Personal Lie* is actually "true." Let´s say they think, "I am a failure," or, "I am not good enough." They will always reach the point where they fail in order to prove that their belief about themselves is true. They will start whatever project, but when they have some success they unconsciously start to sabotage themselves so finally they fail again. Unless one day they find out their *Personal Lie* is, "I am a failure," and start to work on it.

It is so magical to see how people's lives start to change when they replace their *Personal Lie* with their *Eternal Truth*. To free ourselves of this belief is essential to live a life full of satisfaction and purpose. If we live our lives proving the "truth" of the "lie" of our beliefs, we cannot serve our higher purpose. When we come to know our *Personal Lie*, and do the affirmations, and release it by doing Liberation Breathing—then it no longer manipulates us.

HOW TO WORK WITH YOUR ETERNAL TRUTH

Our *Personal Lie* is a belief we have created very early in our life, so we have been thinking it many years. Of course it needs some dedication to repeat and practice the new belief, your *Eternal Truth*. Your *Eternal Truth* is a statement that is the reverse of your *Personal Lie*.

During 30 days you write it down 30 times a day, using the response column (reaction to the affirmations) where you write down each thought that appears during this writing process. It is like a weeding out process in your mind to get out the unconscious and resisting thoughts into the light.

An additional way is to write your *Eternal Truth* (an affirmation which is the reverse of your *Personal Lie*) on little cards and put them everywhere. This way you will see them frequently—like pin it on the fridge, put in next to your bed, write it on the bathroom mirror, lay it in your car, etc. Be creative. You really need to find efficient ways how to get it into your mind easily.

And, the most important, you do private Liberation Breathing sessions to let go of that thought and connect yourself to your *Eternal Truth*. This is really the most amazing experience to transform anything in your life into love and truth.

For me it was incredible how my life changed. That is why I offer other people this opportunity to free their life from the slavery of the unconscious mind.

What is your *Personal Lie*?

In Truth, Simplicity, Love and Service,

Silke

ZEROUM LAW IN AUSTRALIA

My own personal lie can be both subtle and blunt. Writing these words for Sondra also induced my *Personal Lie*. Somewhere inside of me, I think, *it doesn't matter* if I write something or not. (My *Personal Lie* is "I don't matter.") If I don't write something, someone else will. This thought of, "I don't matter," produced constant interruptions every time I came to the computer to write. I have done this for most of my life. Some people would say I am very well mannered, and always put others first, which may appear true, but perhaps underlying this perception is my *Personal Lie* of, "I don't matter." Therefore, I often give opportunities to others.

As I look deeper into how my *Personal Lie* came about, it is really a romantic love story. My parents were working overseas in Fiji when I was conceived. A wonderful surprise they said. With a family already made, I came along five years after my nearest sibling. My parents were in a very good position. An island home with servants, good income, my father was very well respected by all and would be asked to counsel many, from locals to expats, clergy men to military. He was also head of his engineering department taking running water to all the villages on the island and surrounding islands. I was in an extremely loving environment when I was conceived, my family was in a very healthy state of mind.

Things changed during my pregnancy when my mother went for a scheduled checkup. When my mother went to lay on the bed, she saw the bed sheets had blood stains, then the doctors had concerns. My parents decided it was in the best interests of my health, and my mother's health, I should be born in Australia. So my mother boarded a ship, six months pregnant, heading alone to Australia where I was born without complications. A "normal" birth. On our return to Fiji, there was much celebration. A crowd gathered to see the new arrival—and it seemed to me the celebration was more for my father than for me or my mother. Everyone seemed to go out of their way to please my father.

Looking at this story, one can see much love and care, but for years, I held it against my parents. Both my sisters were born in another country, and to me, that made them special. Going to school, I would be attracted to anyone different, especially those born in another country. I had a strong sense of, "I don't matter." Thanks to Rebirthing, I am constantly seeing events in my life as opportunities to clear this thought.

Sometimes my *Personal Lie* will take a back-step, then will reappear. I remember the day, eight years after my first ever Rebirthing session, I was in the garden, and I had a very strong thought come over me, "Where were you?" It was said to my father. "Didn't it matter we needed you?" Logically, it made sense that my father stayed where he was on Fiji. But as a new born, I wanted him to be with me at my birth. I wanted to be with the man I would later see as my hero.

An affirmation which had a big impact on me was, "I matter, because I am matter." This works because God has graced me with a body (matter), which means I matter to God—and if I matter to God, then I must really matter to the master plan and all within it.

Past and present relationships have been very clear indicators of my *Personal Lie* coming into action. My present partner, who has the *Personal Lie*, "I am bad," sometimes tries to make me wrong with certain decisions. According to her mind mapping, if I am wrong, I will feel bad (her transference.) When I see this occurring in everyday life, I see myself give up what I want, and confer to her thinking. I don't go into feeling bad, but I do give up the need to be right or have my way because, "I don't matter." It helps a great deal, my partner and I decided to engage in a holy relationship. We openly voice our observations of each other, to each other, in the hope of recognizing and correcting any negativity.

A FEW CLIENTS' STORIES

Bollywood success: I work in India as often as I can. One of my clients in India is a female actor. When I met this person, she was acting in a show where her character was the focus of the show, yet she was not the main actor. Four "stars" were the main actors. This person informed me, she had never been out of work, but, she had never auditioned for a main part. Her elder brother is a big time movie actor and has won many awards, yet my client had never won an award for best actor or supporting actor. She has won accolades, but never the "big" awards, all because of her *Personal Lie,* "I'm not good enough." This actress, decided to commit to ten sessions of Rebirthing. After her initial ten sessions, she trained to be a Rebirther. After the sessions and the training, she started to get offers for leading roles. At first, much hesitation was felt, but working with her breath and her divine connection, she auditioned for the parts/roles and won the part. She went on to do two major movies before realizing acting was only ever to play out her sibling rivalry, and to feel "not good enough" to her parents. This client, although still receiving offers to act, has gone on to work as a healer, with a successful business in India, and with the help of the internet, across the globe. Today, her success tells her she is good enough.

Working in Asia: Working within the borders of India, and working with descendants from other Asian countries, I often come across women who hold the thought, "I am not good enough as a woman/girl." Many go on to excel in their chosen profession. I am working with a girl from Hong Kong. This girl never feels good enough, so much so, she is now completing her third master's degree, all in medicine. I have only just started working with her, so we shall see how she changes. All the study she completes is in an effort to please her parents. To her, her happiness comes second to that of her parents. I hope during our work together, she feels she has already pleased her parents by being alive.

TOVE JENSEN IN DENMARK:

It was a revelation when I first got to know my personal lie. It welled up in me: "I should not have been here," and I knew with certainty that this belief had been buried deep in me since my birth.

I was the second of twins, and only one child was expected. So simple. I could see how this buried belief had formed my life—my urge to fit in, be accepted and please others, and even some times apologizing for taking up space. When I started to affirm that I am welcome in life, many things changed.

In my work with clients I see the same, when we get to their *Personal Lie*. They feel relief for having found the deep reason for their struggle in life. When I do the *Personal Lie* process with everybody in a group Breathwork Session, the whole energy of the group shifts to a deeper level. They feel liberated!

Much love,

Tove

MONIQUE VAN DEN TOORN IN AMSTERDAM:

My *Personal Lie* goes something like this:

My life was happy as a child. At the age of 12 we moved to another country and the new culture didn't really fit me. I adapted and seemed to be happy but at times I realized I hated myself. I had no idea why and ignored it as we would all do in our family. There were no emotions and we didn't know any better. I think this was considered normal as parents wanted to provide for their children economically and raise them as good citizens for the country after the second world war in Europe.

I moved back to my birth country of Holland as a college student, and it took up until the age of 34 when my unconscious *Personal Lie* started to come to the surface. My housemate left, I had no job and I couldn't handle being on my own. My mind started to drive me crazy and I woke up one morning thinking I should go to the train station and kill myself. I didn't understand the pressure I was feeling and could hardly stay in the place where I was. The death urge was very strong. I became depressed asking for help everywhere. Nobody seemed to understand what was going on. I went through years of therapy and the pressure of wanting to kill myself was at times unbearable.

At one point I started to do breathwork with a therapist who was not trained by Sondra Ray, and didn't know about the *Personal Lie*. It was a way of finding out about Sondra and her workshops and I felt I wanted to go to India to do the India Quest at the Babaji Ashram. The energy of that place, the ceremonies and the teachings, and Liberation Breathing sessions Sondra gave us started to slowly heal me. I literally saw the Ganga River take parts of my past lives downstream as She cleansed me. I learned that my *Personal Lie* was: "I shouldn't be here," which explains why I went through a lot of challenging times. I could finally break the cycle and decide to change the thought and never again become depressed.

For the last years I now feel completely free and master over my thoughts. I love this work as a Liberation Breathing Practitioner, and whatever people need help with doesn't scare me. I can handle the situation as I know Babaji helps us always. I finally surrendered completely to Him and take Him as my guide and teacher. Life is peaceful and I feel confident that everything comes at the right time. Are all my thoughts only positive now automatically? No. I can work on them though, and know life is just perfect as God's will for us is perfect happiness.

Love to all,

Monique in Amsterdam

LUCY PATTINSON IN THE UNITED KINGDOM:

At the time I was conceived there was a lot of confusion between my parents about where to be. My father wanted to stay in Manhattan while my mother wanted to be in England. So I was conceived in Manhattan, born in England, and then we moved backwards and forwards between the 2 places for a few years, with my whole family being confused by the situation. I feel in many ways this was the case with my birth. I had a natural birth that my mother said was "great," and they put me on her chest straight away. This was then followed by separating me into a nursery in the hospital for the next 2 weeks, just being brought to my mother for feeding.

My *Personal Lie* is, "I am confused." This has played out in many ways in my life and disempowers me if I am unconscious about it. The beauty of knowing one's *Personal Lie* is we can catch ourselves dropping into our deeply held beliefs and turn it around. This is a lifelong process. Our deepest negative thought doesn't disappear, but through consciousness and breathing it out, its power can be greatly reduced.

It was a huge revelation when I first learnt this from Sondra Ray 25 years ago, and I still see the enormous impact when my clients "get it" for the first time. Everything seems to suddenly make sense for them. Sondra created truly inspirational ways to delve into someone to discover their *Personal Lies,* which I use again and again.

I recently had a client whose *Personal Lie* is, "I am invisible." This explained his whole life. He never felt noticed, never felt he mattered and he lived in this private world feeling there was no point sharing himself as no one would notice him or listen anyway. He was blown away by having this put in 3 words—"I am invisible." He has since been turning his life around through many Liberation Breathing sessions, affirmations and general awareness. What a joy it has been for me to see his transformation from merely being in touch with his *Personal Lie!*

Lucy Pattinson

PHILIP TAYLOR IN THE UNITED KINGDOM:

While on a Quest in Bali with Sandra and Markus, we uncovered my *Personal Lie* is "I don't tell my truth." And when I tell my truth, "I hurt people," and linked to that is, "My truth does not matter." I also feel weak because I don't tell my truth.

Where it originated from I think (I am work in progress) is from my position in my family. I have 5 siblings who all went on to University level education. Because I had mild undiagnosed learning difficulties, I left the educational system without any University degrees. In addition, my father was articulate with a strong robust personality. Growing up the youngest in that environment, I felt my opinion did not matter—or, my truth did not matter.

How this manifested itself was at 16 I got abused by my boss at work, and I didn't say anything. I just left the job and joined the army. Then in my first marriage, I had 3 beautiful children—but when things weren't right, I kept my truth in, and had affairs until it all ended. My second-long relationship was for 4 years. At the 2-year mid-point I knew it was not where I wanted to be. As usual, I kept my own council and had an emotional affair and let the relationship blow up, literally.

In Bali I had a turnaround when I saw my *Personal Lies* were running me. The turning point was when I began to use these affirmations: My truth sets me free; I deserve to tell my truth; People feel strong when I tell my truth; I can tell my truth kindly; I am able to be much more truthful with myself and others.

I still have the odd relapse, and I still make mistakes, but that doesn't make me a bad person. I really see my own goodness, especially now I have Liberation Breathing as a means for self-correction, and I am well aware of the pitfalls of the *Personal Lie.*

As a breath worker, I have been motivated to help others with these tools, and I encouraged my daughter to attend Sondra Ray's *Loving Relationship Training*. I was able to observe her discover her *Personal Lie*, and then deal with it. For a father, this was a magical moment. Her story is interesting.

Born second of 2 girls she was very happy. When her brother was born an intense sibling rivalry started—with the baby boy of the family getting more attention. Her belief started that she was "not enough." This manifested throughout her life—being helpless, never content with her achievements, until the LRT. With the affirmations, "I do enough," "I have enough," and, "I am enough," her confidence is through the roof and her helplessness is all but gone. Her relationships with everyone improved out of sight from clearing herself of the *Personal Lie*, "I am not enough."

KRZYSZTOF PESLA IN POLAND:

Personal lie: "I am not wanted." (Silke wrote about her experience on this one already at the beginning; I fully agree and comply to it. Here some of my experiences.)

I first learned about the existence of my *Personal Lie* during a training with Leonard Orr, but I didn't pay much attention in it. For the second time, I "rediscovered" it about ten years later during a Liberation Breathing session that I had over Skype with Sondra Ray & Markus Ray.

This time I was really attentive, as it turned out, that this thought was actually much more "powerful" than I had superficially perceived it before—being responsible for the most dramatic experiences in my life. *Personal Lies* manifest in three ways (acting out, overcompensating and projecting), so I also use this order in describing my own *Personal Lie*, "I am not wanted."

1. Acting out (direct manifestations)—conception & pregnancy: The first time it manifested was at my conception and pregnancy of not being "wanted." My parents weren't married and weren't even planning it—they were simply dating. I was unplanned, my mother seemingly got upset with the pregnancy, and my grandmother (her mother) had to blackmail my father to marry my mother—otherwise, I would have been aborted. So I had a very strong will to live.

Birth: I remembered my birth in one of the rebirthing sessions in Leonard Orr's trainings, which was also confirmed by my mother. I was a big baby. My birth came as a heavy feeling of not being allowed to leave the womb, and a pressure from the induction caused by the special drug (oxytocin) at the same time. This "being pressed from all sides—being cornered" scenario had a tendency to recur over and over again during my whole life. It manifested as unfounded contradictory complaints from my mother and grandmother towards my behavior, which made me cry in my room for hours. It was seemingly impossible for me to satisfy other people, especially women. The same experience repeated e.g. in my career—pay raise pressures from the employees, pressure to lower my prices from my clients at the same time; pressure to deliver a better quality to the clients, while giving more leisure and freedom to the employees and partners in my law firm, etc.

Parental disapproval syndrome, school time: There were many dramatic scenes in my childhood, based on the "not being wanted" thought. My father made me feel unwanted, especially when he came home from a long trip (he was a musician, and on the road a lot). Being activated by my grandmother and mother, he acted out his anger by hitting me. Unfortunately, that was the last time we met for the next 20 years, as he was too tense when he came to my home town to talk with my mother about their divorce. That was one of the last memories I had of him for such a long time, which made me feel even more unwanted—in this case, by men.

My grandmother, on the other hand, had a tendency to hit me in my face with her finger tips, while being angry, telling me I was "nothing." That made me feel unwanted by older women and authorities. My mother had a tendency to tell me I was a "heavy-to-raise-child," so that made me feel unwanted by women I loved the most. Also, that made my relationships with women very "heavy." My schoolmates bullied me, which made me feel unwanted by people in my age.

Adult life: The connection between my *Personal Lie* and the biggest dramas in my life became obvious in one of my ex-wife's letters to me. She wrote me a 3-page-long email with only one statement: "I don't want you. I don't want you. I don't want you, etc." It turned out she was abusive and addicted to anger, showing me not only my *Personal Lie*, but also my unhealed relationship with my grandmother at the same time. Attracting people who don't want me, and rejecting people who wanted me was a common pattern I got over with Liberation Breathing / Rebirthing.

2. Overcompensating: As I craved to be wanted, I tried to satisfy other people's needs, often at my own cost. Recently it seems to have manifested through having just enough money to pay everyone around me, but not enough to pay myself, which of course made me really upset. This is the one I work on right now.

3. Projections: As my grandfather was an alcoholic, that caused me to reject him, and project my *Personal Lie* onto him (I didn't want him anymore). Other people I care for have a tendency to "hurt me," which causes me to have a "broken heart" and reject them (not want them) anymore.

These are some of the ways my *Personal Lie*, "I am not wanted," have manifested. Seeing the pattern is a big part of getting over it. Then you have to breathe it out of your cellular memory doing regular Breathwork. I wish all of you "not wanted people" out there all the best! Just remember, LIFE wants you, and you want LIFE—or you would not be here.

Love, Krzysztof

PILLE TALI IN ESTONIA: A DIALOGUE

SONDRA:
Would you be willing to share what your *Personal Lie* has been, and how it has affected your life?

PILLE:
Yes. My *Personal Lie* is that, "I am wrong." And the moment I realized that, all the suffering in my life fell together, like pieces in a puzzle, and I could really understand myself, and my psyche.

SONDRA:
And where did you get that thought, do you think? Were you the "wrong" sex?

PILLE:
Yes. My father was expecting a boy, so I was the "wrong sex" in his eyes.

SONDRA:
And how has this affected the rest of your life, exactly?

PILLE:
Well, it has affected my personal life more. Because only my father was the one who thought I was wrong as a woman, and born as a baby girl, I have an ease in the working area. I have a ease at work with clients, and a very nice relationship with my daughter and me, but with men, I find it difficult. I attract the "wrong men." I seem to have my *Personal Lie* more *activated* around men.

SONDRA:
OK, Thank you. Does it affect your body at all?

PILLE:
Well, ever since I have been studying the *Personal Lie*, and all the theory and magic around it, I have understood that if ever there is anything *wrong* with me, it is always my *Personal Lie* that is down at the bottom of the issue.

Whether it is emotional, whether it is something outside of me, or also if I have a physical illness, of course.
SONDRA:
OK, then anything that is "wrong with you" in your body, you can trace it down to that thought.

What has helped you to overcome it? What has been the best thing for you? Is it Breathwork, or did you do something else?

PILLE:
The first thing that gave me a great relief, myself, was realizing my *Personal Lie*. That is sort of half the job when you realize that.

Then along the way, I have done a lot of Breathwork. And also *A Course in Miracles* has helped me to shift into my Truth, out of my personal sufferings.

SONDRA:
OK, Good. How about any interesting clients who were stuck in their *Personal Lies*? Can you think of any cases?

PILLE:
Well, every person has a *Personal Lie*. So I would say everyone is stuck in their *Personal Lie*. Many have the common ones, like, "I am not good enough," or "I am not wanted," or even, "I am wrong," like mine.

SONDRA:

It would be good for you to figure out the *Personal Lies* of the men you are with, yes?

PILLE:

Yes, that would be really good to study.

MARKUS:

One of the reasons we are writing this book on *Personal Lies* is to bring this information more into the public eye, but also to other Breathworkers who don't necessarily process people on their *Personal Lie*. And we feel it is so important in the process of Breathwork, we want to write a book to help other Breathworkers to be clear about this subject. We feel the main "one thing" to liberate people from is their *Personal Lie*.

You know, in *A Course in Miracles* it says, "Let me recognize the problem so it can be solved," and then it says there is only one problem, and that is *separation from your Source*. But we feel our *Personal Lie* is *the main way* we separate from our Source.

So the main work we have to do with people is freedom from their *Personal Lie*, which is also freeing them from their *separation from their Source*. That's why we feel this is such an important subject. And, we have been trying to write a book about it for a number of years, but finally we have both "dug into it" equally now. That's why we are *on it.*

SONDRA:

Yea, we had some trouble coming up with the right title. The title is **Liberation: Freedom From Your Biggest Block To Pure Joy.** OK, Well, anything else you want to say about it?

PILLE:

I really like how one person who took the LRT (The Loving Relationships Training) said it as a feedback, "Once you realize your *Personal Lie*, and how it is affecting everybody around you—you get so much relief, and so much power and motivation."

Because this is what I am adding from my side, "Life becomes more understandable." And really, the intimacy you have that you really understand another, life becomes a deeper thing.

SONDRA:

So now, having this little booklet on *Personal Lies* will help you when you are finding the right man!

ALL: Laughter !

A NOTE FROM SONDRA RAY
THE "MOTHER OF REBIRTHING"

LIBERATION THROUGH CONSCIOUS
CONNECTED BREATHING

It is not enough just to change your *Personal Lie* to the opposite. Reprogramming in that way is important; however, breathing it out of the cells is also crucial. So this is why we are so happy to have breathwork, the benefit of which gives more oxygen cleansing the cells of the body and restoring them to normal.

In Liberation Breathing, the inhale and the exhale are connected in a relaxed rhythm, pulling the inhale up into the upper chest—into the heart center or sternum area—and relaxing totally on the exhale. The inhale and the exhale merge so that the breathing feels and sounds like an unbroken circle. The inhale and the exhale are relaxed and full, not forced. The breathing is not too fast or too slow. The most important aspect is the rhythm. One can breathe in and out through the mouth or in and out through the nose. We usually start people using mouth breathing so we can hear the quality of the breath and so they can take in more air. This kind of breathing is done mostly in the chest, with emphasis on breathing with the lungs instead of the diaphragm or belly, which has a different purpose.

The rhythmical, circular breathing, done by pulling on the inhalation and relaxing on the exhalation in a continuous, connected stream, empties the negative mental mass from the body and enables you to incorporate life energy into your body. At some point, there is a reconnection to Divine energy, and as a result, you may experience tingling and vibration in your body. This is good! It means old darkness is going out and new energy is moving in.

This breath cycle into the upper chest can break you out of unconscious holding patterns in regarding to breathing and living. It is like a baptism of the Holy Spirit with power. The breath, together with raising the quality of your thoughts can heal almost anything. Because the *Personal Lie* is such an "addiction", you need something strong to push it out. Liberation Breathing has the potential to liberate us from the consequences of thought and place us back into the Mind of God from which we came. At some point we become aware of the subconscious mind activating experiences, and the need for the help of the Divine to clear these unconscious factors. Without the help of a forgiving Divine Intelligence, this clearing would be difficult. Therefore, we have taken the step to "hand over" the process to the Divine Mother. After one has breathed about 45 minutes, we as practitioners read the 108 names of the Divine Mother out loud while the client continues to breathe. Then for completion, we have the client turn on their side and do nasal breathing while we recite a very powerful mantra to the Divine Mother 108X.

The spiritual dimension of Liberation Breathing is the heart of the matter. Connecting the inhale to the exhale merges Spirit with air. It merges the Divine Energy with the physical body in a way that nourishes the nervous system; it cleans the blood and relaxes the organs, as well as brings peace to the mind.

This spiritual breathing is like a biological experience of God. We feel that we have improved Rebirthing by adding the Divine Mother energy. The Divine Mother liberates you, so that is why we now call the Rebirthing process Liberation Breathing. It is the pure shakti power of the Holy Spirit that helps make a radical change. It is the Divine intervention for counteracting entrenched tendencies. People feel safer and go deeper with the prayers and mantras, and we were told it makes the rebirthing process 9X more powerful.

Liberation Breathing takes a person beyond thought itself, into the realm of Holy thoughts and miracles. In India they say the original spark of creation is a feminine aspect. The Divine Mother is the Primordial Power, the Creative Energy. We also invoke the Divine Father energy by working with our Master Babaji's energy in each session. Since we always incorporate A Course In Miracles into the work, we have the Christ energy as well. In other words, we have on the altar photos of Babaji, Jesus and the Divine Mother, Ammachi. This we call the *Dream Team*.

You can go on our website and find out where we are travelling to; but you can also schedule a Liberation Breathing session with us on Skype or Zoom. We are thrilled to be able to offer you a way of liberating yourself from your biggest block.

Love,

Sondra Ray

Liberation Breathing® Sessions
with SONDRA RAY & MARKUS RAY

Book a Session at bit.ly/LBSession

CHANGING LIVES AROUND THE WORLD

HOW A LIBERATION BREATHING SESSION FULFILLS YOUR DEEPEST DESIRE.

I was thinking at the end of editing this book, "What could I say to inspire you to take up the wonderful lifestyle of Breathwork that we have devoted our lives to spreading around the world?"

What could I say to you, our readers, that would get to the heart and soul of your deepest desire, and help you to fulfill that desire?

What is your deepest desire, if I may ask? To be in good health? To be prosperous and affluent? To be fulfilled in your work? To have a loving family? To feel a general sense of Joy and well-being all the time?

Recently I gave a talk on the redefinition of God when we were in Estonia this year. The closest actual definition of God is a Life Force that pulses and breathes through all things. It is the very atom of Creation Itself. It is the "stuff" of the Cosmos, and it is also the Energetic Force that molds and moves that stuff around into beautiful manifestations. And the true nature of this Movement is Pure Joy.

Our deepest desire, then, must be to harness this Power of the Life Force in order to realize Pure Joy, to make ourselves one with an awareness of this Force of Life by which all things exist. Harnessing this Power produces good health. It surpasses most other notions of well-being. Breathwork, Liberation Breathing in our case, liberates you from problems, thoughts, memories, situations that are causing you stress and discomfort. It makes you aware of the Divine Energy that keeps you alive, in a conscious and simple form of deep continuous breathing. You link one breath with the next, in a kind of circular rhythmic flow. The results are remarkable. You take in actually more Life Force. You awaken new potentials in yourself that were previously asleep. You gain a Divine Connection.

Infusing more mana, or what the Yogi's call prana, into your system of awareness, wakes up your mind and body to a new Power. This Power can then be applied to healing, to change, and to manifesting your desires. First and foremost, it can be used to manifest a quiet mind, forgiving of the past, and make you ever attuned to the beauty of new possibilities of the present.

Defining God as the Life Force, Liberation Breathing gets you more in touch with God directly. And this feels tremendous. It changes everything for the better. It puts more oxygen in your cells, and expands them to release negative cellular memory. You breathe out the negative energy that has been held in the cells, and cleanse your cells with new life. You get in touch with thoughts and memories that have been lodged in your subconscious, keeping you stuck, so you can let them go. Breathwork is a matter of maintaining good health and balance in the mind and body, using the breath to make contact with the actuality of the spirit that can heal and balance, release and transmute all negative charges and vibrations in your system.

Sondra Ray was a registered nurse for 14 years before becoming one of the first Breathworkers in the world. In nursing she saw a lot of people working hard to get well, but the truth was they worked even harder to get sick! Liberation Breathing is the easy path to wellness.

If you have got this far and read this book, you have a good idea of the insight that Breathwork, and all the adjunct spiritual practices that go along with it, can bring into your everyday life. It is not some woo-woo etheric occult notion of calling on invisible entities in the sky to solve your problems for you. It is a practical use of the tremendous healing Powers of Breath you already possess in yourself, plus the right use of your mind. Breathwork awakens them to your disposal.

Why don't you try it? We are available for private, one-on-one Liberation Breathing Sessions anywhere in the world. We conduct them live over a conferencing platform such as Skype, Zoom, FB Messenger, or FaceTime. Sessions last about 1.5 hours, but can go as long as 2 hours. You can book a session here: **bit.ly/LBSession.** Give your mind and body a chance to rest and reconnect with the essence of your Life Force, the Energy that created you and all the Cosmos. Connect with the Divine, and fulfill your one deepest desire.

Love,

Markus Ray

ABOUT THE AUTHORS

SONDRA RAY, author of 22 books on the subjects of relationships, healing, and spiritual matters, was launched into international acclaim in the 1970s as one of the pioneers, along with Leonard Orr, of the Rebirthing Experience. She has trained thousands of people all over the world in this conscious connected breathing process and is considered one of the foremost experts on how the birth trauma affects one's body, relationships, career, and life. As she puts it, "This dynamic breathing process produces extraordinary healing results in all of your relationships—with your mate, with yourself, and with Life—very fast. By taking in more Life Force through the breath, limiting thoughts and memories, which are the cause of all problems and disease, come to the surface of the mind so they can be 'breathed out', forgiven, and released."

Applying over 40 years of metaphysical study, she has helped thousands of people heal their negative thought structures, birth trauma, habitual family patterns, and unconscious death urge. She encourages people to make lasting positive changes through Liberation Breathing® to be more free, happy, and productive. No matter what Sondra Ray is doing, she is always trying to bring about a higher consciousness. Recently she has written new books on the subject of *Spiritual Intimacy©* and *BABAJI: My Miraculous Meetings with a Maha Avatar,* and **Physical Immortality**, in which she envisions a shift in the current paradigm in relationships around the world to a new level of consciousness—free from anger, conflict and even death.

MARKUS RAY, artist, poet, and twin flame of Sondra Ray, received his training in the arts, holding degrees from the Cleveland Institute of Art and Tyler School of Art of Temple University in Philadelphia. He is the author of a major work, Odes to the Divine Mother, which contains 365 prose poems in praise of the Divine Feminine Energy. Along with the Odes are his paintings and images of the Divine Mother created around the world in his mission with Sondra Ray.

Markus is a presenter of the profound modern psychological/spiritual scripture, A Course in Miracles. He studied with his master, Tara Singh, for 17 years in order to experience its truth directly. His spiritual quest has taken him to India many times with Tara Singh and Sondra Ray, where Muniraj, Babaji's foremost disciple, gave him the name Man Mohan, "The Poet who steals the hearts of the people". In all of his paintings, writings, and lectures, Markus creates a quiet atmosphere of peace and clarity that is an invitation to go deeper into the realms of inner stillness, silence, and beauty. He teaches, writes. and paints along-side of Sondra Ray, and many have been touched by their demonstration of a holy relationship in action. His iconic paintings of the Masters can be viewed on <u>markusray.com</u> which he often creates while Sondra Ray is lecturing in seminars.

SONDRA RAY'S Author's Portal :

Bit.ly/SondraRay

MARKUS RAY'S Author's Portal :

Bit.ly/MarkusRay

OTHER RESOURCES

Sondra Ray / – author, teacher, Rebirther, creator of the
Loving Relationships Training®, Co-founder of Liberation
Breathing® and Quests to Sacred Sites around the world:

Facebook: www.facebook.com/sondra.ray.90
Facebook Fan Page:
www.facebook.com/LiberationBreathing
Twitter: www.twitter.com/SondraRay1008
YouTube: www.youtube.com/SondraRay
Website: www.sondraray.com

Markus Ray / – poet, author, artist, Rebirther, presenter of
A Course in Miracles, co-founder of Liberation
Breathing®
Facebook: www.facebook.com/markus.ray.169
Facebook Fan Page:
www.facebook.com/LiberationBreathing
Twitter: www.twitter.com/MarkusRay1008
Website: www.markusray.com/
Receive Markus's weekly articles on ART here:

"Art Look" – an art lovers companion –
www.markusray.com

Sondra Ray & Markus Ray
301 Tingey Street, SE
Washington D.C. 20003

E-mail: contact@sondraray.com
E-mail: contact@markusray.com

Babaji and The Divine Mother Resources:

Babaji's Ashram in Haidakhan (India)
E-mail: info@haidakhanbabaji.com

Haidakhandi Samaj (India)
E-mail: Info@HaidakhandiSamaj.org

Sondra Ray & Markus Ray
on these Websites:

www.sondraray.com   www.markusray.com

www.facebook.com/LiberationBreathing

We encourage you, our reader, to attend The Loving Relationships Training (LRT) which is produced by Immortal Ray Productions all over the world. You can see Sondra Ray & Markus Ray's worldwide teaching schedule on:

www.sondraray.com/programs-seminars/

Also, we encourage you to attend The INDIA QUEST, The BALI QUEST, or other Spiritual Quests that teach and disseminate Liberation Breathing practices, and principles of *A Course in Miracles*, as well as enhance your Divine Connection to various Spiritual Masters. These are also available on: www.sondraray.com

Artwork and paintings of the Spiritual Masters by Markus Ray are available on: www.markusray.com

COME WITH US ON A QUEST TO SACRED SITES !

112

NOTES

Printed in Great Britain
by Amazon

10436954R00084